REMEMBERED BY HEART

Aboriginal and Torres Strait Islander people are
respectfully advised that deceased people
are referenced in this publication.

REMEMBERED BY HEART

FOREWORD BY
SALLY MORGAN

FREMANTLE PRESS

Publisher's note: Variations in spelling are
consistent with the original publications.

Every reasonable effort has been made to obtain
permissions for all copyright work. Please forward
enquiries to Fremantle Press.

First published 2014 by FREMANTLE PRESS
25 Quarry Street, Fremantle, Western Australia 6160
www.fremantlepress.com.au

Cover illustration by Sally Morgan.
Cover design by Ally Crimp.
Printed by Everbest Printing Company, China.

National Library of Australia
Cataloguing-in-publication data is available on request

ISBN: 978-1-922089-77-9

Government of **Western Australia**
Department of **Culture and the Arts**

Fremantle Press is supported by the State Government through the
Department of Culture and the Arts.

CONTENTS

FOREWORD

The Native Welfare controlled every aspect of your life in those days. It was very hard for Aboriginal people then and I learned very young that I'd have to be determined if I wanted to get anywhere.

Elder Joan Winch

This moving collection of youthful memories touches on a broad sweep of history and includes people from many different Aboriginal countries. The stories have been shared in the hope they will make a difference to people's understanding of the past, and in the belief that a just future can be created for all.

These are powerful stories of survival that share pain, humour, grief, endurance, life experience and hope. Taken as a whole, they detail the devastating impact of many decades of repressive legislation on the lives of individuals and families. Legislation which, while aimed at 'protecting' Aboriginal people, obliterated any access to basic human rights.

By 1911, each state and territory in Australia, except Tasmania, had passed legislation giving government officials absolute control over the lives of Aboriginal communities. The powers granted under the various Acts made it possible for officials to legally control people's movements. To this end, areas of land were set aside as reserves, government settlements and missions. Aboriginal people were forced to live in such places. Segregation was further supported by the criminalisation of acts of resistance. In Western Australia, it was a criminal offence to resist internment on a reserve or settlement. Leaving a place of internment without first obtaining permission left an individual open to prosecution and arrest. Nationally, the far-reaching powers of the various Acts ensured segregation was a reality of life for Aboriginal people in Australia. Elder Hazel Brown recounts the experience of her mother:

> *My mother was brought down from Carnarvon on a cattle boat. They kept them down in the bottom of the vessel and didn't let 'em come up top. It was a rough trip and they all got sick. From Fremantle they took 'em to Balladonia Mission, and then a few weeks later took 'em all the way to Carrolup. The white people musta thought they were gunna try to run away back to where they come from.*

In Western Australia, it was the *Aborigines Act 1905* that sanctioned the removal of Aboriginal children from their families, providing for their institutionalisation — often thousands of kilometres away — in missions, settlements and reserves. This process shattered families and communities, disconnecting people from their country and culture and leaving a legacy of confusion and despair that is still being dealt with today. Stephen Kinnane, whose grandmother was removed under such legislation from Miriwoong country in the Kimberley, writes:

> *They did not see the hole they were tearing. They did not see they were taking someone's daughter, someone's grand-daughter, someone's sister, and someone's future mother. They studied my grandmother, but they did not see her and they did not see the chain of events they were setting in place.*

The rationale for removing children from their families was often based on the need for education or the provision of better living conditions. With few exceptions, the education was minimal. Girls were trained to be domestic servants, boys to be farm labourers or station hands. In addition, while the living conditions in places of internment varied, they were often worse than the situation from which the children had been removed, supposedly for 'their own good'. Elder Alice Nannup was removed from her family at twelve years of age and sent to Moore River Settlement. Alice's mother had been a wonderful cook, and Alice records her disgust at what she saw when asked to help out in the settlement kitchen.

For the soup they'd cook up these awful sheep heads. First they'd skin them, but never take the eyes out, then they'd split them down the middle, give them a quick rinse and throw them in the copper. Sometimes those sheep heads had bott-fly in their noses but they wouldn't worry about that. They'd just throw it in and we'd see that in our soup.

The stories in this anthology reflect the changing times and policies over the decades. Historically there had been a view that Aboriginal people were a 'dying race' and it was only a matter of time before Australia's Indigenous population would be extinct. When it became clear this was not the case, that rather than decreasing, the Aboriginal population was increasing, government administrators became fearful of what they termed 'a social menace'. In 1937 the Conference of Commonwealth and State Aboriginal Authorities decided that 'The destiny of the natives of aboriginal origin, but not of the full blood, lies in their ultimate absorption by the people of the Commonwealth ...' Consequently, in the late 1930s government policy moved in the direction of assimilation. The ultimate aim of assimilation was the extinguishment of all cultural ties between Aboriginal people and country, the end of the kinship system, the death of law, language and identity. In other words, cultural genocide. In practical terms, this meant the lives of Aboriginal people were even more tightly governed. *The Bringing Them Home* (1997) report notes:

> *... assimilation was a highly intensive process necessitating constant surveillance of people's lives, judged according to non- Indigenous standards.*

David Simmons, a Nyoongah person from the south-west of Western Australia, comments on his own consciousness of such surveillance.

> *In 1951 the Native Welfare Officers were still active. My younger school days were occasionally spent hiding from the Native Welfare. My mother insisted that I go to school, but there was always that dread that I would never come home from school because of Native Welfare.*

Tjalaminu Mia, also a Nyoongah person from the south-west of Western Australia, recalls the suffering she experienced under the assimilation process, while living at Sister Kate's Children's Home.

> *Its aim was to turn lighter skinned Aboriginal kids into white citizens and I suppose it was part of what used to be called the White Australia Policy, because the politicians of the day wanted this land*

*to be white. It was a very racist policy because they
expected us to forget all about our families and our
culture and take our place in white society instead.*

The deep thread running through this collection and linking each story with the next is one of pride. Pride in family, community and survival. Pride in being Aboriginal. Bronwyn Bancroft captures this in the final paragraph of her story:

*I am proud of who I am. I am proud of where I've
come from. I'm proud of what I've done and I'm
proud of where I'm going.*

Anyone reading these stories will come to understand there is a lot for each person in this collection to be proud of.

Sally Morgan, 2014

REMEMBERED BY HEART

Stephen Kinnane

TRACKS

My grandmother's skin was concealed when she was a small child. I am of my grandmother's skin. Her skin leads to my mother's skin, and my mother's skin to mine. My skin is olive and supple. Cuts do not heal quickly but dissolve slowly into raised scars devoid of pigment. The scars last. They show. But this is not the skin I am talking of. I was reunited with my skin when I returned to my grandmother's country, Miriwoong country. *Jalyirri* is my skin. It is how I am placed. It is my skin of reunion. My grandmother was placed by her skin, *Nangarri*, and then taken away to a place where her skin meant nothing more than colour.

A dissecting black border was ruled north–south through the Kimberley, slicing my grandmother's country in two. It cut its way along Empire-red maps dividing the northern frontier into federated Western Australia and the Northern Territory. White people had been in my grandmother's country less than twenty years when she was born. The Europeans saw these countries simply — pastured or rocky, fertile or infertile, inhabited, but from where they stood, under utilised. They saw only two seasons in the East Kimberley, Wet and Dry. The Dry is seen as hot and dusty. The Wet is even hotter, but the heat is broken by the rains. The Miriwoong identify four seasons: Rain, Cold, Windy and Hot. Come the Rain season the country sings into life in rich greens, reds and purples. There is plenty of food and it is Law-time; time to catch up with the mob and rejuvenate the land. The ground is always damp, and can become one vast glass-like flood plain when the afternoon rains thunder down.

Tracks are harder to follow come Rain time. In the Windy season it is cooler and there is no rain. Life swells around the larger water supplies where there's food and business. Tracks last a long time in the dry red earth and the nights are clear and fresh. But the ruling *guddia* saw the world only as wet or dry, black or white. Within a world of 'Empire' they marvelled at their clinical brilliance. They had reduced the world into discrete, simple particles of matter. But it is not so simple. My grandmother's skin had held the story of over two thousand generations of her people's life in their country and then the generations of others. She was born of the crossing of this vertical black line. It cut through her country and into her life.

My grandmother was broken down into 'authentic' parts, half white, half black, but never seen as wholly human. She was the product of the Colonial Frontier to be mapped, traced, labelled and categorised. They called her a 'half-caste'. They thought they had her pegged. But then they didn't know what to do with someone who didn't fit within their neat lines of demarcation so they decided to remove her from their picture. When they took her away they thought they were solving a problem. They thought they were setting the picture straight, clean of their own sins, free of imperfections. They did not see the hole they were tearing. They did not see they were taking someone's daughter, someone's grand-daughter, someone's sister, and someone's future mother. They studied my grandmother, but they did not see her and they did not see the chain of events they were setting in place. They did not think she would remember what had happened to her, or that others would share in this story. They did not think we would one day be leafing through the personal files they created about our grandmother, watching back, as her life was tracked and controlled across those pages for almost half a century. Cuts leave scars. Scars leave tracks. Tracks can be followed.

Lake Argyle stretches the walls of what was once the giant Ord River valley. Tourist brochures boast that it is the largest man-made lake in Australia, containing nine Sydney Harbours nestled neatly within paperbark-covered hills. It is classified as an inland sea, an unnatural version of the ancient sea that 'explorers' had coveted and mythologised as they searched in vain through an imagined landscape. In reality it is neither a lake nor a sea. A concrete and rock dam wall wedged in a gorge on the Ord River tenuously holds back this enormous body of water.

Today, beneath the massive lake's surface the land lies transfixed, cold and silent. Like the hull of a giant sunken ocean liner, my grandmother's country lies trapped in time, holding the memories of thousands of lifetimes, and a moment of disaster when the waters flooded in. If you turn south at the ruins of the old homestead though, and search along the silty floor, you will pick up a trail. These are my grandmother's tracks leading silently out of her country. Although it is dark beneath the silent waters and the tracks are very old, look carefully and you will see them leading all the way back to a place called Wild Dog.

Friday 29 June 1906. Wild Dog Police Station. Before they took her away my grandmother's name was Gypsy. She had been taken off a cattle station called Argyle. My grandmother's older half-brother's name was Toby. He had been brought into Wild Dog from the Ord River Cattle Station, which was further south. They waited together. Gypsy was recorded as being five years of age and Toby as being six. They could have been older. They could have been younger. Over the years their ages would fluctuate across the pages of the files that were created about them as figures of authority took wild guesses about their beginnings. For certain, they were too young to be away from their families. They were two small children being held over by the Kimberley police pending their removal. It was all matter-of-factly noted in the Police and Aborigines Department files. The lean sentences, tidy phrases and abbreviated words of bureaucracy were used to begin their story. A simplistic system was in place to decide their future. Although the sentences might be spare, reading these records is like deciphering a code. To be chained and dragged a hundred miles was described as being 'escorted'. To live in a camp with your family was deemed to be 'neglected'. To have fairer coloured skin than your mother meant 'suitable for removal'.

Government enquiries into the removal of children use dates in their calculations of the numbers of Aboriginal kids taken away from their families. The dates coincide with the passing of legislation when this practice was proclaimed legal. However, these official dates are arbitrary and misleading. From the time the guddia first entered this country Aboriginal children were taken. To really understand what happened, and how it impacted on the lives of Aboriginal communities, you have to listen to stories that have been handed down.

I passed around my grandmother's photograph in the park in Kununurra, the one of her soon after she entered the Mission. In the photo she was a chubby little five-year-old.

When she smiled her eyes were all squinty in the sunlight. She was short for her age, fair skinned, big hipped and skinny legged. She had a big birthmark on her left thigh, and a head that was too big for her body. She was a funny-looking little kid, and she was a long way from her home. I wasn't sure if it was permitted to show the photograph so widely, but Nangala said enough time had passed for cheeky spirits not to be a worry. The photo was of great interest and all the women had cooed and sighed, and laughed too, at the sight of my grandmother dressed up in mission clothes.

My grandmother and her brother Toby were some of the first children taken from the East Kimberley by government authorities, but not long after them the yearly toll started to rise. Many of the women sitting in the park had experienced the trauma of having their children taken away. Some of them were younger than my mother and had had their children taken from them as recently as the 1970s and 1980s, when they were sent as babies to Princess Margaret Hospital for treatment, and once there were adopted out without the women's consent. I think this is one of the reasons why they were so welcoming; it was not just about my grandmother, but about every child that was taken away. I could come back and be placed because missing children and their stories are not forgotten. One aunty told me she is still waiting for her son to come back. It is the same in the south, where too many older women waited their entire lives without ever being reunited with their children. This is our community history and an unresolved daily reality for many Aboriginal families.

The Swan Native and Half-caste Mission had been operating in the village of Middle Swan for at least seventeen years when my grandmother and her brother arrived. On the morning the SS *Bullarra* docked at Fremantle, the children were met at the wharf by the missionary Miss Jenny, who ran the Mission along with her sister, Effie Mackintosh.

Perhaps given a coat or something warmer to wear, the children were taken by steam train on the long journey to Midland Junction. I can't imagine what they made of the train, of its steam, its size and its thunderous noise.

Built on a pastured ridge, in cleared bushland, the Swan Mission grounds sloped gently towards Jane Brook, which swelled with paperbarks and reeds. Beyond the brook, hidden by the paperbarks and accessible by a muddy track, were the much more substantial buildings of the Swan Boys Orphanage and St Mary's Swan Parish Church. Although possibly the first establishment at the site, the Swan Native and Half-caste Mission would always be the poorer of the two institutions, hanging on at the fringes and beyond view.

It was winter in the south when my grandmother arrived, and she and her brother were placed in the dormitory with thirty or so other children. Being infants they were able to stay together for a time. It was Mission policy that when boys reached the age of seven they were transferred to the nearby Swan Boys Orphanage with the white boys. The girls remained at the Swan Mission House.

The children at the Swan Native and Half-caste Mission had come from all areas of the state, and their removal to the Mission coincided to some extent with the colonisation of Western Australia. As the colony spread from the South-West through the Midlands to the Gascoyne, out to the Goldfields and eventually into the Kimberley, the names of children being removed from these areas reflected this expansion. Children were renamed Cue, Gascoyne, Linden, Argyle and Menzies. The names were registered at the Mission in parallel with the growth of towns and stations of the same names as white settlement spread and more children were scooped up by the police. With the rapid expansion in the north, from 1905 onwards the population of Swan Mission was increasingly made up of Nor'wester children like my grandmother.

Gypsy from Argyle Station, along with her brother Toby, was given a new name. The baptism was a ritual of renewal as well as destruction. Their older names and skin names were replaced with English names and they were forbidden to ever use their language again. Gypsy was renamed Jessie Argyle. Her brother was renamed Thomas Bropho.

Children who were removed from their families learned to form special bonds with other Mission children, bonds that were to last a lifetime for my own grandmother. Separated from family, country and homeland culture, the children of Swan Mission survived by adapting as best they could. But that isn't to say they lost all sense of an Aboriginal framework of belief, respect and belonging.

Where you came from and who your people were became especially important to children taken thousands of miles from their homelands and people. In your own country, rules of belonging were clearly defined and understood. With the disruption to this constancy the children held all the more defiantly to their sense of country. Skin defined you within your own culture, and as the missionaries worked to wipe any sense of skin from the children's minds it became even more important to know where you were from and who else was from your region.

Out of the pain of removal, Mission children learned to claim as extended family people from country in the same general direction as theirs. Skin was replaced by a sense of your country, and those from similar country became your countrymen. In broader terms the children divided themselves into Nor'westers and Sou'westers. It was a system the missionaries tried to replace with a sense of belonging in the church, but while some children no doubt acquired a sense of the God of the Christian church, they were also aware of other spiritual and cultural belonging linking back to their homelands.

Nor'westers were kids from Carnarvon and further points north, including those from the Goldfields to the north-east. Sou'westers were mostly Noongar kids from the south-west who had been removed from their specific homelands but still remained within Noongar country.

My grandmother was taken from the new world order of the guddia in the East Kimberley to the new order of the missionaries in the south. Children from different Aboriginal countries were forced together under a singular fixed ideal of a Mission education that was supposed to equip them for a world of servitude and piety. They were influenced by their home cultures, by other people's home cultures, by the church, by their removal and by the situation they found themselves trapped within.

The Mission was supposed to be their new family, their new homeland, their new culture. It was supposed to be a place of Christian teaching and obedience. It was this, but with the addition of the children's own different senses of belonging, the culture of the Mission became far more complex, dynamic, and even contradictory than the missionaries were able to realise. The children might have prayed to Jesus daily, but at night they feared spirits that dwelled in the fertile Noongar country outside the dormitory windows.

Swan Mission received subsidies from the state government on a par with other white institutions of the time, marking it out as unusual compared with the New Norcia Mission to the north, which received far less for the children in its charge. Nevertheless, the children still had to contribute to the working life of the Mission to make it a going concern. When Thomas Bropho (Toby) turned seven, he and my grandmother were separated. He was sent across to the Swan Boys Orphanage to sleep and to receive schooling, but would return after his three hours at school to help with the chores around the Mission. The same went for Jessie (Gypsy) and the girls who lived their entire day at the Mission House. The younger girls had to learn to sew, cook and serve dinner and, as they became older, to care for the younger children. They had to tend the orchard, milk the cows, feed the stock, collect the eggs, and generally help run the place.

After a long day's work the children were locked into the main dormitory. Single beds stretched in rows down either side of the long red-brick building that cut west from the main Mission House where the missionaries slept, meals were prepared and lessons were carried out. It was a place of planned repetition designed to breed well-mannered, hard-working, obedient children who would take their place — and that was never expected to be too high a place — in white society. They did learn, but not beyond what they had to know to be good workers. They ate well when the Mission was doing well, and sang for their supper, literally, to raise funds to keep themselves afloat. The place was small enough not to be overwhelming, but large enough for the children to separate into groups of Nor'westers and Sou'westers.

It was the kind of place that was greatly affected by the staff who ran it, and for some of my grandmother's years there, there were some staff members who were particularly good. Sadly though, for some of those years there were staff members who were particularly bad.

The children soon became attuned to the regular rhythms of a Mission life of work and prayer, and within a short time of James and Letitia Jones' arrival, escapes decreased. In that period the new girls' dormitory was also completed. Photographs were taken of the sturdy new walls lined with iron cots down either side of the corridor of highly polished jarrah floorboards. It looks like a hospital ward. Kapok pillows sit on crisp cotton bedspreads with neat tassels that the girls would have sewn and embroidered themselves, and you can just make out the high and wide, heavily barred windows separating the neatly hung pictures of Christ.

The Joneses allowed the children to head bush on Sunday afternoons to hunt, cook food in hot ashes and scout the country. The inmates loved this chance to get out into the bush. It seems to have been some kind of recognition by Mr Jones of the children's culture, and they appreciated it. Beyond Mr Jones' desire that the children really understand the Bible, and that they really embrace Christ; beyond the repetitious rhythms imposed by these desires, the children were also operating from their own rhythms — watching for *jennuks* (bad spirits), and checking out each new inmate to see where they belonged; to see if they were from their home country.

Of the many people who managed the Swan Mission, Mr and Mrs Jones were the only ones that my grandmother remembered fondly. Among the people I have spoken to from the Mission and the stories that have been passed down, the Joneses were remembered for being solid, fair-minded people. My mother tells a story of when she once met them, years after they had left Swan Mission, on a visit with my grandmother. The Joneses had a small farm in the Perth hills and my grandmother was given a tour of the orchard and enthusiastically invited to sample fruit from every tree. She wasn't allowed to leave until she did.

I decide to try and track the Jones family down. I know that it isn't possible for either Mr or Mrs Jones to still be alive, but I am curious about what happened to them. Registrar-Generals' records in the archives lead me to death dates. Obituaries in the newspaper lead me to the married names of their children. The Joneses' deaths, their children's marriages and their addresses begin to link up as a paper trail, and I begin building my own files on the people who entered my grandmother's life. Shipping records and biographical indexes take me back in their story to when their ancestors arrived here, to the journey that would bring the young Mrs Letitia Jones, and the not-so-young Mr Jones, to the Swan Mission to answer their Christian 'calling'.

Tracing them back, I want to go forward and track them across electoral rolls and through telephone books. A good thirty calls later, some distant family are revealed. This branch of the family has photographs of the Mission and they give me the contact details for a woman whose name I recognise. She was the youngest daughter of the

Joneses, who the children in the Mission referred to as 'Baby Jones'.

In a well-tended suburb of the city, widowed, and not exactly sure of what I want of her, was the woman I will call by the name my grandmother used, Baby Jones. Baby Jones is eighty-six and she looks well for her age. The child of missionary parents, she grew up in the Swan Mission separated by a brick wall from the girls' dormitory where my grandmother and thirty or so other young children slept. She has agreed to give me her time and to tell as much as she can about the Mission. She agrees for me to use a tape-recorder so I won't forget the details of what she has to say.

Baby Jones' story is carefully filtered by her fear for her parents' reputation. She is guarded because there is much talk in the newspapers of the Stolen Generations. She doesn't like that term. She doesn't think it represents the real situation as she sees it. As we talk I realise there is a bigger stake here. Baby Jones became a missionary herself and worked in other countries, and I believe is worried that all that she has worked for is under threat. In some ways, it is. It is the fate of all of our histories to be scrutinised by later generations. But as she becomes more relaxed and realises that I am not here to attack her, that I am genuinely interested in her history, she shows great pleasure in remembering the many Aboriginal children of Swan Mission who she claimed as her friends.

She remembers back to the time when her limbs were

wiry and supple and she ran without fear of anyone or anything, where the world of childhood seemed as natural as breathing. As a child she had shared the same air, played in the same orchard, hauled up gilgies from the same creek, and looked for love from the same woman as the Mission children had. Washing with the Mission children, eating with the Mission children and being punished with the Mission children is how she describes her upbringing. They were friends of her own age and she remembers them with a great sense of affection.

'Oh dear,' Baby Jones says, as she looks at the photographs of the children that I have brought with me. 'That's Tommy Bropho, my coachman.' Each morning Thomas had taken her in the sulky, over the river, beyond the brickworks and the grounds of the Orphanage, to the state school where the white children received their education. Each morning, barefooted, but without a stitch out of place in his heavily mended clothes, Tommy took the young Baby Jones to a place where he was not allowed to go. If she is aware of the obvious difference between her privileges and Tommy's situation, she does not mention them.

Baby Jones is peering at the images as if they will somehow begin to move. But the images don't move easily for her. It is a long time back that I am asking her to remember. The names have a bit of difficulty coming to her, even if she recognises their faces. 'Ah, this is Bob Dorey, he was my little friend.'

Baby Jones remembers her adventures with Bob

Dorey. She remembers how the Mission creek would flood in wintertime, right up to the horse's chest as they tried to cross the river, and how they'd hunt for gilgies every weekend. Out of school, and after chores, they were free to roam the grounds, dig for roots and bake fish in ashes on the river bank. She remembers 'Ception (Conception) and Chattra Benjamin milking the cows, filling the pails for the day. Queenie Magnet is watering the vegetables. Thomas Bropho is gearing up the horse and buggy and the Parfitt girls are getting sulky, 'jumping the traces'. They'll be brought back into line by her mother, Mrs Jones, she says with a knowing smile.

After a slow start the memories come flooding in. Dion Dirk is checking the chicken coop for any eggs to feed the little children and Mrs Jones is keeping an extra special eye out for little Mary in case she fits again, due to her epilepsy. When she tells me this it jogs my own memory of a story my grandmother told about Mary fitting in the dormitory, and how the older girls learned to look after her so she did not swallow her tongue.

Baby Jones remembers learning to milk the cows and polish the floors, which were always kept so shiny you could see your face in them. She can see her father, an older man, who had travelled the world from the age of nineteen. His bout of malaria, which nearly killed him, turned his hair white for the rest of his life. And she can remember my grandmother, Jessie. 'I can remember her quite well. When you said her name, yes, Jessie Argyle,

I could make a mental picture of her. I can see her quite plainly, what she looked like. She used to have long hair, fair skinned she was, and very sturdy.'

She sees them sitting outside on a summer's night. The Mission children are all gathered in the evening dusk. Mr Jones plays his gramophone, seated in his wooden chair in front of the children who are sitting barefoot on the grass in neat rows. The strains of the 'William Tell Overture', the 'Huntsman's Chorus' and the 'Ride of the Valkyries' waft out over the orchard and settle in the paperbarks that strangle the creek.

Baby Jones says she loved her time at the Mission. It gave her some of the happiest memories of her life. She believes there was really no difference between her upbringing and that of the Aboriginal inmates. She says she ate the same food, cleaned as they did, played as they did and attended church as they did. To her it is a story of racial harmony and equality.

Baby Jones does not seem to realise that she was not one of them. Simply by having her parents, she was not one of them. She got to keep the name her parents had given her and live the choices in life they would make for her. When she turned sixteen she would not be sent out as a domestic servant.

Baby Jones is surprised to hear that Uncle Bob Dorey is alive, and a little defensive as she asks, 'And what was his story?' A moment of relief sweeps over her face as I tell her he remembered her parents fondly, but not the people before them. Uncle Bob had remembered Baby Jones with affection too.

But Uncle Bob has his own memories. They are of a different place, though it is locked within those same grounds and occupies the same space. For him, the Mission is viewed from a perspective which could never really be called home. It is a place out-of-country. This is not to say that Baby Jones' version of her life at Swan Mission is invalid.

In tripping over the threads of the past you have to respect the experiences of witnesses; you cannot confuse one telling of a story as the only telling. In the battleground of the Mission where hearts and minds, cultures and races were up for grabs, stories of friendship are always welcome. But they aren't the only narratives that affected these children's lives, and to ignore the story of servitude that was set out for them is to ignore too big a part of the picture.

The children were trained to serve God and Jesus, to serve the white people who had taken them from their homelands and replaced skin, country and family with the wafer-thin pages of the Bible. Their lives revolved around lessons, work, survival, and the slow movement towards their exodus into a world that they had only made small excursions into since leaving their home countries.

Abridged from *Shadow Lines*
Stephen Kinnane, 2003.

Alice Nannup
LIFE IN MOORE RIVER

The time came for us to catch the train to Mogumber and we all felt really excited. We knew nothing about Moore River, hadn't heard much about it. All we knew was what they told us; that we were going to a mission. To us, we thought we were going to a place where there'd be lots of lovely little kids and that we were going to be really happy. Well, what a joke that turned out to be.

We got to Mogumber siding at about one or two o'clock in the morning. We got off the train and onto this old truck to go the eight mile ride out to the settlement.

When we got there they unlocked the dormitory to let us in, then showed us to our beds. Doris and I had the two beds in the middle. When we got in we could hear all this whispering, like little kids talking. We didn't see Herbert again for a while because he was stuck over with the boys.

The next morning when I woke up I could hear birds singing. I peeped out from under the rug and all I could see were these little faces looking at me. I thought, ooooh, what's this. I'd never seen so many faces

Anyway, we got up and went to have a wash. We never wore nighties in that place, we just slept in our shimmy and pants. We went off to wash our face and comb our hair, when all these kids came across and asked, 'Where you come from?' I told them we came from Roebourne and they didn't much care about us, just walked off. See, they were South girls, they were all from country in the South.

Then these other girls came around and said, 'Where you come from?'

'I come from North,' I told them.

'Oh well,' they said. 'We come from North too.' So the North took over then and looked after us.

On the very first morning we were there we were taken up to the office. Mr Brodie was the superintendent then, and his wife was the matron.

They spoke to us for a while about the rules and things like that, then Matron asked me if I knew who my father was. I told her yes, I did. Then she asked me, 'Do you know the Flinders?' and certain other people from Roebourne. I told her yes because they were all my father's friends. In fact, Mrs Flinders said that if she had known I was going to be taken away I could have stayed with her and gone to school with her three daughters in Roebourne.

Anyway, this questioning went on for a while, and then

they let us go. But afterwards they always called me Cassit. Matron would come along and she'd say, 'Cassit! Cassit! Cassit! Don't you go past me when I call you.' I'd look at her and say, 'I'm not Cassit, I'm Basset,' but she'd never call me by my proper name.

It used to eat me a little bit, but then I found out that Mr Brodie had been a policeman up in Roebourne. See, they probably didn't like me having my father's name because he came from such a big family up there.

Well, now that I saw for myself what the settlement was really like, I just gave up all hope. I thought, there's no way I'll be going back home now.

Moore River was split into two main parts; the compound where all the kids and older girls were, and the camps, where all the married people and old people had to live.

The compound was set up just like a little town. At the bottom end of the main street was the Big House — that's the superintendent's quarters — and this faced the church which was at the top end of the street. In between, on either side, were all the other buildings, like the dormitories, dining room, sewing room, bakehouse and staff quarters. It was built up on a ridge, and down on the flats near the river were the camps where all the campies built their little places.

The superintendent and his wife were the head workers there. They had five sisters: one for the surgery, one for the dining room, the sewing room, the school and the girls' dormitory. There was also a second boss who was in charge of the stables and fencing, outdoor things like that, and a third boss who went out with the woodcutters.

There were black trackers for policemen too, both Nor'westers and Sou'westers. But mostly they were Nor'westers because if they did anything wrong up on the North, like killing a bullock, they'd be sent down south away from their country. Their main job was to catch anyone who ran away, and they used to wear these old police uniforms with the brass buttons pulled off.

Us kids were all put up in the compound and it was a rule that we weren't allowed to go down to the camps. They always tried to keep everything separate there. There were separate dormitories for boys and girls, and even to go into the dining room we were kept separate.

The dining room was shaped longwise, with the boys having steps up one way, and the girls having steps up the other. It was really horrible to eat in there because the cups and things were that dirty, and we had all these old tin mugs and plates left over from the First World War. The food was terrible; that's the food we ate, not what the superintendent and white staff had. They had beautiful food; roasts, lovely stews, curries with rice, food like that. I know because I ended up working at the Big House, and they certainly didn't have to eat like we did.

At dinnertime we used to have this soup, only I couldn't eat it because it was just like dishwater. None of us could eat it, we'd just try and pick through the best of it. We used to make up on the semolina — that's what they used to give us for breakfast — no sugar on it of course. We'd have semolina and a piece of bread'n'dripping for breakfast. Well that would be our fill for the day because we couldn't eat the soup.

One day I was asked to go up to the kitchen to relieve because one of the girls was sick. Luckily I only had to do it twice; I couldn't stand what I saw there. The food for the compound was cooked by the girls. They'd have one of the nurses — well, they were all called nurses — up there instructing the girls. There were two coppers: one for the soup, and one for the tea. The water would be all boiled up in a copper, and they had this great big shearer's teapot, with tea stewed and stewed up in it.

For the soup they'd cook up these awful sheep heads. First they'd skin them, but never take the eyes out, then they'd split them down the middle, give them a quick rinse and throw them in the copper. Sometimes those sheep heads had bott-fly in their noses but they wouldn't worry about that. They'd just throw it in and we'd see that in our soup.

It was all so dirty. You'd think those nurses would have been more alert, could have done things properly. But they didn't care. I suppose they were told, 'Just anything will do those natives.'

I couldn't eat the soup before I worked there, but when I saw this I definitely couldn't eat it. See, I wasn't brought up like that. My mother was a beautiful cook and we ate lovely meals back home. I think they did things like this to deliberately lower us; well, degrade us really.

The girls' dormitory was an old weatherboard place with a verandah halfway around. It had all different wings under the one main roof. The mothers' wing was out on the verandah at the back, and around five or six of them would be there at a time. See, most of the older girls that went out to work were pregnant when they came back in.

Inside the dormitory was the little kids' dorm, the washroom, and the other two parts were for the rest of us girls. We were all locked in at night but the doors between each wing were left open.

In the girls' dormitory we had an old matron-mother, old dormitory mother they called her. We called her Nanna Leyland, and she was a beautiful old lady you know, but strict too.

She'd be next door in a room to the side, and she wouldn't yell at us if we made any noise, she'd use her stick. She had a big stick, and she'd hit the wall three times. I tell you what, you'd hear a pin drop. Then you'd hear her coming across the floor, walking stick going; toong toong toong.

When she got to the door she'd say, 'Galahs live outside — people live inside. I'm looking after little kids next door and they need their sleep. If I hear another word I won't hit the wall, I'll come in and crack every head in this room. So just keep quiet.' And she would have done it too!

Just off the side of our dormitory was the pan-room. In there they just had the one night pan for all of us, and we had only enough room to wriggle our way in and sit down. It was in our part of the dorm and sometimes the girls used to come in a hurry and mess the floor trying to get there in the dark, poor things. It was usually the little ones, and for the rest of the night we'd have to walk on water.

On the windows of the girls' dormitory they had wire mesh to stop you from getting out, and a trellis around the verandah. Although they always locked the girls' door, the boys were left free. The boys used to come and talk to the girls at night through the window, but if Matron or someone came along they'd run underneath the building to hide. When the superintendent woke up to what was happening, he had a stone wall put around the bottom of the girls' dormitory to stop the boys from hiding underneath.

Even though Nanna Leyland was really strict, she was a lovely lady to us too. When I got in favour with her I used to live like a queen. See, she used to give us her dog, Brindle, to go bush and get a kangaroo for her. There'd be me, Melba, Ruth and another Melba, and we'd go out along the river hunting, just us girls, taking the butcher's knife and everything. Then after we'd given her the brush kangaroo, she'd make a beautiful big stew and a damper for those girls that did the hunting for her. She'd bring in that special food at night, because even though she had her own camp outside, she was always locked up in the compound at night.

Sometimes, too, we used to go across to old Bill Kimberley and old Mary — that was the policeman and his wife — and they'd have a bit of brush kangaroo or something. The boys' dormitory was built up high, you could walk right under it and sit down, and that's where Bill and Mary lived. They just had a few sheets of iron put this way and that, and they'd have their fire out in the open. See, where the girls had Nanna Leyland as a dormitory-mother, the boys were kept in line by one of the trackers.

Some people liked the trackers and some didn't. It's just the same as every other place I suppose. My mate Dorothy didn't like Bluey, they just couldn't see eye to eye. He used to stand at the door to the dormitory and usher us girls in, and Dorothy would have a go at him, you know, give him a good stir. So she'd be there stirring him up, and one day he said, 'Dorothy Nannup, get in that formatory or I'll hit you over the stick with a head!' Well, look, we just roared laughing, she didn't have an answer for that. I tell you, we used to have funny little instances like that. It never used to be running smooth at all.

That old Bluey had a vegie garden and he used to supply the compound with soup vegetables. The girls used to sneak down, get in there, and pinch a few of these vegies. They'd tie their belts tight and stuff carrots, turnips or whatever they could get down their tops. Then they'd crawl through the fence, get across the river and wash them, then have a good old feed. They'd bring some back to us too, to have in the dormitory when we were locked in at night. See, we were always hungry, but I'd never do anything like that — I just couldn't.

Life in Moore River had a real routine to it. Every Saturday morning Sister Stewart would line us all up, boys on one side, and girls on the other. She'd stand at the top of one line and another sister would stand at the other. They'd have these big chemist bottles full of Epsom salts and everyone would get a big glassful. It'd be down with the Epsom and then you'd get a lolly to wash the taste away.

We hated it, and instead of getting in the front of the line we'd all push to get at the back. But sooner or later it would be your turn, and I tell you, they'd make sure you swallowed it all before you got your lolly.

We also used to have drill down on the playground. That was just like the aerobics they do today. The playground was just a big sandy area on the flat, behind the church and next to the boob. The boob was the prison. We'd wear the same clothes for that, nothing special, and usually it was the schoolteacher who took us. I don't know what the big girls did, whether they did drill somewhere else, but this was only for us younger ones.

We had to play sports too, and I used to like playing boys' hockey. We never had proper hockey sticks though. We used to go down the river and find crooked sticks, then put them in the fire so they'd tighten up. Sometimes we'd get wire and tie it on the end to make it look like a real hockey stick, and we'd run around having a good old time.

Doris, Herbert and I were sent to Moore River in August, and the first Christmas we had there was in 1925. I always remember that Christmas morning because these beautiful voices were singing, coming down from the church. I woke up and heard these beautiful voices floating down over the compound. 'Doris, Doris, quick, wake up,' I said. 'The angels are coming!' I really thought it must have been angels to sound like that.

All the girls in the dormitory jumped up and went to the verandah. The dormitory was all blocked off with a trellis but we could just see through to the outside. I looked and saw these girls standing out there in the middle of the street, between the two dormitories, singing.

It was the girls' choir, and I could see the two Darby girls, Dinah Hall and several others. They sang, 'Christians Awake' and 'Oh, Come All Ye Faithful'. They really made the ranges ring, and that's the only time Mogumber was ever beautiful.

I was going to school in the settlement up until that Christmas, and for a couple of months after. But I can truly say that they never taught me anything in all that time.

I'd finished up to grade three at the school in Toolbrunup, and that was as high as Moore River went. So when the teacher was busy she'd get me to go out and keep the infants occupied while she taught the bigger class.

Moore River did nothing for me by way of schooling; I had to learn through experience and picking up little bits here and there on my own. Really, all I ever did there was work. I had chores to do before school and chores to do after. I tell you, they never allowed me to be idle.

I was still going to school when they decided to show us

a movie. We all went up to the church, men and boys on one side and girls and grown up ladies on the other. This was a Charlie Chaplin movie and you know how funny he is.

Nanna Leyand used to always wear this hat and her and a couple of the old ladies were sitting in front of us. A lot of the people there had never seen a movie before, especially these old ones. Anyway, the thing went on, flickering away, when this motor car came full ball down the street towards us. Poor old Nanna went, aaarrrgghh, and ducked right down. Oh, look, it was such a laugh, funnier than the movie. Every now and again this motor car would come around the corner and Nanna and these old ladies would duck. Us little girls sitting behind her were killing ourselves laughing, but we couldn't laugh out loud or she would have thumped us.

That's the only movie I can recall them ever showing us. We had a couple of slide nights too, religious ones, but those soon fell by the wayside.

I hadn't been at the settlement long when I got a letter from Jessie Hornsey. Miss Greenwood had married while we were with the Campbells and her name became Mrs Hornsey. When we were at Pallingup we used to ride over to her place and do odd jobs. Anyway, she wrote to me and asked if I'd come and work for her. Mr Brodie knew all about it, because everybody's letter that was written into that place was read before it was given out. He didn't say anything to me when I got the letter but he called me into his office a couple of days later.

'Do you really want to go and work for Mrs Hornsey?' he asked.

I said that I'd like to because she'd written and asked me.

'But,' he said, 'you can't go because we've got another job lined up for you.'

Well I don't know what that job was but I never went to it. I think they just wouldn't let me go to Mrs Hornsey's because they wanted to disconnect people from their past. I was still at school at this time, but not long after they needed girls in the sewing room so they put me there to work. So whether that was the other job he was talking about or not, I don't know.

All the girls who were taken out of school and sent down to the sewing room, were started off on button holing and things like that. We had no choice about working there and we were never paid for it. We'd work a full week, then we'd go down every Saturday morning to clean the machines, brush them and oil them up ready for Monday. Then they'd come along with a little block of chocolate for us and that was our pay.

Every so often, Mr Neville, or an outside visitor, used to come up to the settlement. Whenever Mr Neville came everything had to be spit and polish — we'd have to really clean the place up, and sometimes we had to get into lines for when he arrived.

The best thing about someone from the outside coming was we'd get to eat better food, something special, in case whoever it was came into the dining room and had a look around. But this was only once in a blue moon. I remember hearing around the place that the Prince of Wales wanted to come up to the settlement but Mr Neville put him off. 'No,' he said. 'You don't want to go there. They're cannibals.' I don't know if this is true — it's just what I heard.

One time when Mr Neville came we were all in the sewing room, and he was standing talking to the sewing mistress. They were talking about education and other things, and I heard him say, 'Ohh, it's all right, as long as they can write their name and count money ... that's all the education they need.' Well, I think that tells you all he thought of us.

When I think back to the time I spent at Mogumber, I think about how they always had me working, never left me free. Every morning I'd get up and go to breakfast, then I'd go straight over to the office. A boy named Edward and I used to work in the store weighing up the rations — like sugar, tea, flour — and handing it out to the camp people.

When Nanna Leyland came to get her rations I'd always put a little extra in and hand it over myself. I gave her a tin of baking powder once, just a little tin. I stuck it in with the flour so you couldn't see it. Sometimes I'd give her a little bit extra rice or salt or whatever, because that's how we would work it. She'd have extra and then she'd cook something to bring into the dormitory and feed us at night.

After I'd finished up in the store in the mornings I'd go straight down to the sewing room. Then at about five o'clock I'd be finished there, and I'd go up to the office to trim the lamps. I used to do the lamps for the girls' dormitory — they had to be trimmed every night and put in each wing before tea.

One night I finished trimming the lamps and I took them off to the dormitory. When I got there a girl was standing on the steps waiting for me. She was deliberately blocking my way, so I looked up at her and asked her to please get out of the road. She moved aside, but when I walked into the room she shoved me in the back. I didn't take any notice of that, I just walked into the dormitory and took all the lamps to their different places. But as I was walking out she stood in the doorway.

'You've been talking about me,' she said.

'You?' I was surprised.

'Yeah me, and what have you got to say about it now?'

'Oh,' I said, 'tell me what I said about you then?'

'I know what you said about me.'

'Well then, you tell me.'

But she wouldn't tell me, so I told her to get out of the way, and she hit me. So I up and hit her back, I gave her the works. She was a bigger person than me, too, but I just lost my block.

There was another girl sitting there and she said, 'Come on break it up, you two.' But I was angry and I wouldn't stop.

When I did let her go I said, 'You tell me who told you I was talking about you?'

'Ruby Windy told me,' she said.

'All right,' I said, 'I'll go and bring Ruby back.'

As I was walking down the steps to go and get Ruby I said to her, 'Are you going to face Ruby?'

'No,' she said.

'Why?' I asked her, but I knew why. 'Well,' I said, 'you've got to face her,' and I walked off around the corner.

When I found Ruby and told her she was furious. She came back with me to the dormitory, walked up the steps and said to this girl, 'When did I tell you this?' Well of course she couldn't answer, so Ruby lifted her too.

Then the girl who had told us to let off fighting butted in and it was a free-for-all. It ended up us telling them that if they wanted to find anything to make a fight over, they'd better make sure they knew what they were talking about. See Ruby was a Nor'wester — she came from Carnarvon — and all us North people stuck up for each other. It was that kind of a place, you just had to stick up for one another.

The North and the South would have many a fight you know, they were terrible. They'd fight rather than have a feed — just like the Irish and the English. The two sides were a very strong thing. Northies were anyone from Carnarvon up. See, someone would make up a story that wasn't even worth talking about and it'd spread and spread, until it was way out. Then that would be passed around and, before long, there'd be a fight over it.

One thing I was lucky about at Moore River was I never got a beating. Lots of girls got a thrashing but I never did.

They used to take them down to the storeroom and the superintendent would belt them until they weed all over the floor. They never spared them, and in the afternoons I'd have to go down with a mop and mop it up.

So for those that got punished, the punishment was harsh. If girls ran away they'd send the trackers after them and they'd be brought back and their hair would be cut off, then they'd do time in the boob.

At the sewing room we used to make clothes for Forrest River Mission, and for Moore River as well. They never had to buy clothing for us, we made it all. It was terrible material too. But if you were a good worker, at Christmas they'd give you a piece of good material and you could make yourself a frock. Me and another girl, Dorothy Nannup, were really favoured — we used to get a piece and we'd make ourselves something nice to wear.

One morning me and Dorothy stepped outside to get into line for church and all these boys looked across and wolf-whistled and shouted. We had our new dresses on and they reckoned I was a butterfly and goodness knows what else. My dress was a plain one, but Dorothy, she made a flarey, flouncey one. When she'd spin around it would twirl out. Mine was more of a plain Jane sort of thing, but still, I made a good job of it.

Although there were awful things that went on at the settlement, and once you were there you were there until it suited them, good things used to happen too. I used to really enjoy going to church, and I loved swimming down at the river. Another one of the things I liked was going to the dances they held once a fortnight. The compound would have our dance on a Wednesday night, and the campies would have theirs on the Saturday.

Everybody looked forward to these dances. We'd wear the dresses we made, and get electric wires and do one another's hair. Olive Harris was a good friend of mine and we used to go off to Nanna Leyland's, or down to old Aunty Pat Rowe's, and sit by the fire warming up our electric wires. When the wire gets hot enough you curl your hair around it and you end up with ringlets or lots of curls. Matron used to give us some hair clips, and we'd all get dressed up for the dance.

These old fellas from New Norcia — Charlie Bullfrog and Ben Jedda — used to come over. Old Charlie played the piano accordion and Ben played the violin. Oh, Ben was beautiful, he used to make that violin talk, and we'd all just get stuck into it. We used to love square dancing too you know. Four here, two over there and two there, and you promenade, and do this that and the other. Oh, it was beautiful. We enjoyed it so much we'd be saying, 'Oohh, come on Wednesday night.'

Abridged from *When the Pelican Laughed*
Alice Nannup, Lauren Marsh and Stephen Kinnane, 1992.

Hazel Brown

GROWING UP AROUND NEEDILUP

The first children taken to the Carrolup Native Settlement from around Ongerup were Clem and Anna Miller, Lily and Fred Wynne, Fred Roberts. Would've been about 1914. They took 'em from Toompup; got Bonnie Jean Woods too. Their great-aunt was looking after them. Most of their mothers had died.

Fred Roberts and Fred Wynne ran away from the settlement in 1916. People there got terrible treatment, and the black trackers who did all the bossing of the inmates were really brutal. They used and abused most of the young girls, and the real fair girls nearly all took husbands just to get away. Sometimes the girls ran away, but they tracked 'em down and brought 'em back.

The old people lived in camps on the other side of the river, and the young boys and girls were locked up in dormitories every night. People weren't fed properly, and the young people had to work, but pay or money was never heard of. They buried people wrapped up in chaff bags, and a lot of them died when they shouldn't have, because they didn't get medical treatment. Nearly all the babies were born in the camps.

The dead bodies were kept in the jail, a big mud and stone building with only one window with a thick wooden door and a big bolt and padlock. If you didn't do what they ordered, they locked you up in there, with the bodies.

My mother Nellie came with Maggie Williams, Daisy and May Dean. They were all taken from their mothers up in the Murchison area. My mother often told me how the girls were treated in Carrolup. She was unhappy and always afraid. They didn't always understand the ways and laws of Aboriginal people down here. Another five cousins joined them a few weeks later, and that was better. Better for her, anyway.

My mother was brought down from Carnarvon on a cattle boat. They kept them down in the bottom of the vessel and didn't let 'em come up top. It was a rough trip and they all got sick. From Fremantle they took 'em to Balladonia Mission, and then a few weeks later took 'em all the way to Carrolup. The white people musta thought they were gunna try to run away back to where they come from.

My mother did run away, but they caught her and made her marry my father, Fred Yiller Roberts. He had quite fair skin, they reckon. She was fifteen years old.

She died in 1975. She never ever saw her mother again. Most of the children sent down from the north married, and not many of them ever went back to their own people.

Different times now, they say.

When they were little, my kiddies were asked if they wanted to go there for the holidays. You know, Community Welfare ran a holiday place down there for children. But even though they've changed the name to Marribank ...

Well, for the years they ran the Carrolup Settlement ... well, just the name, it sickens you. They've changed the name, but none of us ever forgot that it was Carrolup. To us that was a concentration camp. And that was somewhere we had a fear of, and didn't ever want to be sent.

I remember Lionel Howard, who had been taken away from his own relations and didn't know why as he hadn't done anything bad. He came back to Borden, only to be caught again by the police and taken back to Carrolup.

He used to tell us many years later of the treatment he received there, and of the food they were given to eat, and how they were locked up in the night and flogged by the black police whenever they spoke up for their rights. He had a special hatred for these black police, and I remember one time telling us he was glad they were all dead.

Lionel was able to run away from Carrolup again and never ever let the police catch him after that. He was always very timid and frightened of the police and Native Affairs people.

Well, there was a lot of people like that ... There was a lotta reasons to be frightened, for us to be careful, you know, back when I was young.

We moved around the Borden, Ongerup, Gnowangerup and Needilup area until I was about four years of age. Then we came back to Gnowangerup to live, about 1930. That's when Freddy Yiller died. My mother then had two children, so Fred Tjinjel Roberts — really the only father I've known — he married my mother.

They got legally married about two weeks after Fred Yiller Roberts died because that was Noongar way, you know. She was accepted Noongar way, and his brother died, and so he had to look after her. He had to care for her, and for us. And then about ten months after, my brother Stanley was born. We were living on a reserve, oh about half a mile from the township. Brother and Sister Wright had a mission house about two mile away.

On this reserve where we were living we had an old tin hut that served as a church and a school. And they had a hospital. It wouldn't have been half as big as this room, and I can remember it well, it had an open fire. My mother used to act as a midwife, and look after the women when they had babies.

If you lived in Gnowangerup you got what they called the government rations. The government gave the missionaries flour, tea and sugar, and tobacco, to share out among Aboriginal people, see.

We stayed in Gnowangerup for a while, and then Daddy said, 'Well, not worth staying here, we might as well go somewhere else to raise the kids and give them a better life.'

Daddy took us out to Needilup. Dad used to go around the district shearing in the season, but we stayed at Charlie Brown's farm, and Dad worked all through that district.

Daddy used to go out and set snares for kangaroo, 'cause you could sell the skins, you know. You used to get about one pound ten (they used to call it thirty shillings then) for one good skin.

He used to skin the joeys too, and peg 'em. Mummy used to scrape the skins and tan 'em and cut 'em into squares. She used to make blankets. Well, they ran out of cotton thread one day. We used to buy it in big reels.

'Ah well,' I said, 'can't do any more sewing.' We used to sit down and watch Mummy sew and sew. She used to make blankets and sell them to farmers and travellers, you know. That sort of helped us keep going.

But there came this time when the thread ran out.

So she used the sinew from a roo tail. They cut the tip of the tail off, and they pull it, and when the tail comes out this sinew comes out. You pull it all into pieces, make it like cotton, and dry it. Sometimes before you dry it, they twist it on a bone. When it's dried it's just like thread anyway.

And Mummy used to use that to sew the blanket.

She had one big needle like a darning needle. And Aunty Ellie said, 'You know you can make that needle.'

'How?'

They used to have oilstones, rasps, axes, three-cornered files.

'Well,' Aunty Ellie said, 'I'll show you how.'

Mummy didn't know how to do this, Daddy didn't bother to show her, and neither did anyone else. She didn't have to do it before she met my father.

In a kangaroo's arm, there's that long, skinny bone. Anyway, Aunty Ellie got one. She filed it right down, filed it right down. Made it real skinny. Then with the corner of the file, she made a hole in it, for the thread to go through.

She made Mummy two, three of them.

You could do that out of hard wood too. Aunty Ellie used to do that out of sandalwood. Make a needle, make the point, and then burn a hole through the head part. Then you pull the thread through. She used to do it with sinews, too. She used to make us boots out of the kangaroo tail, and moccasins, you know.

She'd sit down and scrape the skins. Nothing was ever wasted. Used to sit down and take the sinews out of the tail, and use the boomer skins and that to make the carrying bags.

Noongars were very efficient, only because they were taught by their people. It was more or less about survival.

And in 1935, Mum was pregnant and we went back to Gnowangerup. And she had my brother Aubrey.

After Aubrey was born our family consisted of four kids, and we went back to Brown's. We had relations all round, we used to see them at Christmas time. Browns were terribly good white people, because Daddy had been working with the two Brown brothers ever since they came back from the war. We stayed at the Browns until 1936.

In 1937 we went back to Gnowangerup. I used to go to school with the white children; Aunty Mag and Lenny and myself went to school. Audrey was born then.

The Aboriginal people had shifted from living on the reserve near town, most of them. There was a block of land about three miles from Gnowangerup, and Sister Wright made a mission there. And Audrey was one of the first babies to be born up there. I think she was the third baby to be born at that particular place. Well, we stayed there then and Daddy used to go to Borden and shear all around. Around 1938 we stayed in the mission and went to school. We stayed and my mum had treatment for her bad eyes.

We'd been at the mission before, right at the very beginning of it, for a few weeks. This was even before the people started to build the mission house. We planted a lot of trees which are still there today.

My mother knew Sister Wright when she was back at Carrolup, and she wrote her a letter and told her there was a lot of Aboriginal people in the district, and how the ones she had made friends with had asked her to let this good Christian white woman know that they all would welcome her and wanted her to come and help them as all of them wanted to live as free people.

Brother and Sister Wright lived in Gnowangerup for all these years, and saw many of our people born and grow up and die. There was over two hundred people at the mission, everybody was happy, and the children went to school and Sunday School. The men worked all around the district; the ones who didn't find work picked wool and sold it to buy food and clothes for their families. I went to the mission school with my two brothers. Most of the girls and teenage boys went to work as soon as they left school. Those days you had to work hard and the pay was always poor.

Lots of times the boss from Carrolup — Mr Bisky, he drove a brown Ford car — would come and want to take away some fair children or perhaps a widow or someone who done something wrong.

Brother never wanted them to take kids and that. As soon as anyone used to come down in that car, Brother Wright always knew. They couldn't come on the mission because that was owned by the church, and they had to have Brother Wright's consent to come there and look around. They wanted women that had no husbands, or children that had no mothers, or the fair ones.

But Brother always knew that he was coming. Sometimes he'd come to the school and make an excuse. Maybe he'd say, 'Teacher's not well today' — we only had but one teacher — 'so you can all have the day off' — and he'd go down to the camp, all around on his old pushbike and say, 'Now I want all the big ones to take all the little ones away, and you boys to act as watch' — you know, lookouts — 'take 'em into the scrub.'

Or better still we used to take them into the paddock. And we stayed in the big scrub there, and there was a dam there. And then the mothers'd cook up food and the big boys'd bring it.

The big boys'd stay around, play football or pretend that they were doing something but always keep an eye on that car and where that man was and when he was on his way. And Brother'd go with him as far as town, come back, get on his pushbike and go out to the boys and say, 'Well, he's gone, youse can all come home now.'

All the time, we had that fear. Sometimes, when we used to see the police come in a horse and cart, come up in a sulky, we used to all go and hide, thinking oh well, if you weren't working they'd get you. I used to work sometimes in town, with Mum, before I went to the Richardsons. My mother used to wash all over the district. Down there with the MacDonalds for a while.

If they found a girl was not working, the police would come, take the girl away. That man in charge of that settlement, he always found excuses, you know?

Even if, say, someone used to run away with someone else's wife and they'd go and tell the police. Well, that was a criminal offence. They'd take you away to the settlement for six months or something.

Brother Wright had some Christian friends who had a timber mill down near Manjimup, a timber town called Wilga. This was where the timber was sent to from Gnowangerup mission and our men paid Brother whatever money they could afford for the timber, and also for the iron for the roofs. So cottages were built on the mission; one or two rooms, and much better than bag huts.

Aboriginal people were not allowed in Gnowangerup town after six o'clock. We weren't allowed to go to the pictures and the women all had to have their babies in the camp.

In about the early forties the government gave money for a two-ward maternity hospital, which was built on the mission and it was really nice. All the people were happy at the mission and Brother Wright ran a little store where the people could buy food and he protected the Aboriginal people all the time, always.

But the townspeople and other people made complaints, reckoned that Brother Wright was making profit from the Aboriginal people, and the mission got closed down.

All he was doing was buying the wool people plucked from dead sheep. He gave them a reasonable price for it.

Christian people used to send second-hand clothes to

the mission but, well, not many people wanted to have charity. It sort of made you feel independent if you could pay something for things.

He'd maybe sell a good dress for about tuppence or thruppence or something like that. Well, when people had the money they bought things that they needed and I couldn't see that that was robbing anyone.

And while Brother and Sister were there, conditions on the mission were really good. You had proper medical attention. Well, Dr Boyd used to willingly give that. And Sister used to get medicines, ointment, and eye drops and ear drops. But, those days, not many children had runny noses and bad ears, I can say that for a fact. Very few of them did.

Runny noses and that only came about when people started living in the houses with concrete floors. But Brother and Sister really helped, you know. The kiddies went to school regular. Brother Wright used to ride a bike around to every camp and you had to explain why you weren't at school.

Brother had a dam built there and that was clean water. The women carted water and washed at the dam. They washed their kiddies and they washed their clothes and everyone wore white sandshoes and socks to Sunday school. We only had the one-room church and that was crowded with people.

People loved to be looked after. Brother, he preached a lot, and he was a Christian, but we accepted that, a lot of people accepted that. The living conditions were really good. Some people used to have a garden. When they got their little shack, you know, they used to show pride in it, in their place, the little home that they had. But the government wanted them at Carrolup; that's why they said Brother was robbing the people.

Well, they were getting something for something at the mission. Because whatever they sold — the dead wool and that — they bought food. And they were sort of independent and even the men used to ride pushbikes to work. Brother used to fix up the old bikes and sell 'em, and when people were sick at Borden, Brother used to get in the old car and go and pick 'em up and bring them in. The only help people ever had was Brother and Sister.

After reports were made to the big bosses in the Native Welfare department that Brother Wright was robbing the Aboriginals in Gnowangerup, Brother and Sister were forced to leave. It seems to me they wanted Brother and Sister Wright out so they could close that mission down. Their place was taken by Mr and Mrs Street, who built dormitories. Then only the children of school age had to be looked after by the Streets and all the parents had to go back into the bush to live and find work where they could and fend for themselves.

Well, then they all drifted away, and Mr Street looked after the kiddies and that. And, well, they had no other place to come to, so Main Roads said they could shift back to Gnowangerup, to a place just up from the railway station. That was the old reserve, where Brother founded the first old mission.

Well, they went back there and they all camped around. Tents and bag huts and bush camps and such like. They had to go and leave the little homes that they'd built up at the mission, just to come back and live under the trees again. Well, there weren't any trees, just bushes. I guarantee there wasn't a tree at that reserve that was as high as a kitchen table. So really, they had no home, they were sort of shuffled to and fro. But all those years, they kept their tongues behind their teeth.

They didn't talk, most of 'em, because they were afraid to speak out. The police walked roughshod all over the top of 'em, and did what they wanted and not one said one word.

Abridged from *Kayang & Me*
Kim Scott and Hazel Brown, 2005.

Alice Bilari Smith

IN THOSE DAYS

I was ten years old then, when Walter Smith started teaching us. We were always in the house, in the homestead. We want lolly. We was willing to do anything for him. We started off feeding the chooks. Chooks used to be about half a mile from the homestead. And then we used to go and feed the sheep — the killer we used to have in the yard. We used to go and feed that one, put water and everything, make sure they okay. Then we come back to do a bit of sweeping round the house, outside.

And then when we was turning twelve he tell us to start watching him cooking everything, baking in the oven. We started like that, baking things. He didn't make us work, we just worked for him. Then he started giving more jobs then; we keep going now. Teach us more and more. He used to chop all the meat in the butcher's shop, and he used to fill that baking dish, and we had to go and put it in the cooler. We used to do all them things for him. He used to tell us to go and get vegies — might be cabbage or cauliflower or whatever he needed to cook. We used to go and get it and he used to tell us to chop it up and put it in a pot, cook it.

You might go to the homestead and first it might be wood-chopping time; chop the wood, fill the wood box. We used to use the axe, chop all the wood in the wood heap. If the men were too busy, well we have to chop it, the girls. Sometimes middle-aged womans chop it, and we used to cart it in the wheelbarrow to the homestead. Fill the wood box in the wall outside, to use it for cooking. We had a big wood stove, two-door, so we can fit everything in there, roasting meat or baking bread. We used to bake six bread every day, big loaves of bread in a long tin. We used to bake that with yeast — we used to make it in a bottle all the time. Nice bread, they used to make. Sometime we made a damper, baked it in the oven.

Len Smith and Walter Smith taught us how to cook whitefella way, and waitering job, and sweeping floor with a broom, and baking bread and cooking roast in the oven. How to go and butcher the sheep, and washing up dishes. My mother was started like that, then when we got big enough we used to do the same.

We used to milk the cow every morning, and boil the milk. And we separate the milk from the butter, and we saved the milk in the cooler. There was a big cooler at the homestead, the sort with flywire around it, and a big shallow dish full of water on the top and he overflowing all the time on to the cloths hanging down all round. Keep it cool, all the meats and things, nice. Butter and things wouldn't go bad. We used to wash it inside all the time, keep it clean, put the new lot of stuff there. Might be four shelves that all the different foods got to be on. Meat in there, and whatever vegies you've got for use, from the garden.

Some of the older ladies, they were there too, teaching us. We used to make the soap ourselves — washing soap — from fat. The boss showed them how to do that, and now we used to watch them doing it, all the old ladies. We used to melt the fat — sheep fat, rendered — and put it all in a big tub, like a big bathtub, but specially for the soap. Let it get a little bit cooled down. We mixed caustic soda in water, half a four-gallon bucket, mixed it with the melted sheep fat, and we had to stir it up till it got hard like custard. We leave it for a night then. In the morning we come back, and this big thing's set now. We had a table with a wire in the middle, and a rail, and we cut it all in slices — long ones first, and then we turned it around and cut it in little blocks. We used to make about forty in that one tub.

We used it to wash clothes, the old people's clothes and the bosses'. We never had washing powder like today. When we were washing, we had a washing board — the glass one — we scrubbed it on that. Then they used to boil the clothes in the copper. When you put them in the rinse, you put the blue in the white rag, leave it in there, let him stop and make the water blue. It's good, rinsed out all the smell of that soap. Face soap, that you wash yourself with, he used to order that one. We used to get the round one, nice smell, but you can't get that one any more.

We had irons you put on top of the stove — you might have three. You used one, and put him back to get hot, and you used another one. We only had that one, nobody had electric one. We used to iron the clothes for the two bosses there, Len Smith and Walter Smith, and my father Alex Stewart.

Walter Smith taught us to sew and cut dresses. Say you wanted to make a dress, he used to show us how to fold the material, and where we had to cut, and where we had to put the waist and things, and the hem on the bottom, and the collar. He's the one that taught us. He had no wife. For the bosses, we used to just sew all the buttons and things. In those days, we never had elastic, they only had buttons. We used to sew the buttons, and even a broken shirt that might have got ripped when they were galloping and chasing, we used to sew that. He used to teach us to sew them, patch it up. Any old clothes, get a patch and patch it up. Whatever thing, it had to last for a long, long time, because there was no shop there. Every bit of thing we had to look after them. Not like this time, wasting everything, just going in the dump.

And we used to sew for the old grannies. We used to look after them grannies. Every time when they need something, we might get a material and make a dress for them, or skirt, whatever is. Sometime we make a blouse, but most of the time they like that shirt belong to the men.

Whatever men and women and girls and boys that were working, we cooked food for them all in the homestead. Bread and things, we used to bake it in the homestead. We cooked one lot of meal for everyone, white and black, and he used to carve it all. Put them all in the plate, even the meat and everything, cabbage or carrots, whatever we got. We used to have a dish to take it home, never sit down there. We used to put it all on the dish and go and give it to the men waiting, might be in the big boughshed there. The men were only there for might be twenty minutes and they're off again, see.

But in the homestead, we might be the waitress, we got to work with the two whitefellas. Get everything, set the table and things, get all the food ready for them before we go out. All the rest of the women go out with the food, but we got to wait till we set the table, and when they're sitting down eating, then we get our meal, take them down. We might go home and come back; we clean up the table, wash the dishes and everything. By eight o'clock we finished for the night.

And all the granny and grandfathers, they get a ration, and we used to make a camp fire and cook for them. Walter Smith used to look after all the old people. He used to give all the old people rations free, from the homestead store every Sunday. A little bit of flour, sugar, tea; just from Sunday to next Sunday. Jam, treacle, honey, for the old people. He treated them like that. That's why all the people from the other places come there — they know they get everything free.

They wait till we fellas come, the old people. Sometime if we got any left over from the men's, we used to give it to them. We don't have to cook it then. We used to have big billy like a bucket, boiling: cup of tea all the time. And damper, sometimes we baked it in the camp oven, and sometimes we buried it in the hot sand. Fireplace just in the ground there. Make a fire just in the ground, but you've got to get a special wood so you haven't got ashes, so that meat can be cooked nice and brown. We used to get snakewood — that's really good to cook everything. Nice taste, too. Every morning clean the fireplace. When we finish cooking we bury it in the sand. In the morning we clean it and put a new lot of wood in, and then start cooking again. For sleeping, we had separate fires, near the camp where you go to sleep. We didn't sleep by the cooking fire. You had to make a little fire each side, for sleeping.

The Smiths were very good people. Soon as someone tell them that Welfare coming, he used to tell us to go down the river now, stay in the bush when the Native Welfare coming round, because they going getting all the children, the half-caste kids, take them to Perth. He used to tell us to go bush for a day. We used to be lucky we had a good boss — he don't want we fellas taken away from the mum, from the country. We used to be hiding in the river. He used to go, 'Come on, take it bush.' 'That flash car still there?' 'No, that's gone.' Hamersley and Mulga Downs, all the kids gone. That was about 1930s, that's when it started.

Those days we was very scared about the policeman. We know what sort of policeman been early days, see, when the first Aborigine people and the whitefellas met up about 1870 or 1880, they was fighting. They used to take them away to Rottnest Island, over spearing the whitefellas and things like that. That's what happened before, long time ago, before I born. We still got that in the mind. We know what the families been go through, all the old people, early days. If we do the wrong thing we know the policeman pick us up and take him lockup. We think the policeman pick them up, take them for good, see.

Holiday time, we used to go out bush, and we used to do our own way, Aborigine way. About four or five mile away from the station, where the holiday camp belong to the old people, we used to go. No windmill around; we were near the Beasley River, where the water is, and sometimes a rockhole. The proper name for that river is Maliwartu. They know, old people; they goes make a camp there. Now, we're living in Roebourne, we're staying here forever. But the old people used to keep moving. Wherever the meeting, they go to the meeting, and all the tribe meet up there, different ones.

We took a spring-cart and a camel; when it's getting late we leave the camel and the spring-cart, we make a fire, get a kangaroo, cook him. Catching the wild food, and doing cooking in that grinding stone. We used to cook a kangaroo in the ashes, and we used to get wild potato and things for damper. We only had a kangaroo dog for hunting, no gun. The wild onion is really good; we used to mash it up raw and put it in the ashes, and he come up like a damper. And we used to get a goanna, cook it. That's all the bush tucker belong to the Aborigine people.

I used to watch the old people doing it and I learned from there. They teach me tribal law belong to whatever tribe, and they tell me all the different tribes and that I'm Banyjima woman, I not allowed to go over to Kurrama or any other language. I got to wait for them to invite me before I can say something about the Law that belongs to them.

No blanket, just dig the sand and make a fire each side and sleeping in the sand, and get up in the morning. Summertime not bad — wintertime you got to have something to cover you up. Before the blanket come, we used to use the paperbark tree from the river. Make a fire each side in the camp where we going to sleep, dig the sand and cover us up with the sand.

If a big general rain coming, two or three days one, we go stay in the cave, because we haven't got a tent and things. We used to move to the big caves in the hill near the river. The old people had special ones they know. Whatever things we had there, we got to take them all up to the cave, stay in the cave for two or three days. Doesn't matter we got clothes and blanket and things, we used to put our blanket and things in the cave. We used to get spinifex and make a bed, so nothing would come up and bite the children. We'd take the food, put them all on the shelf in the wooden dish, keep it dry. When they go out, they cover them with a leaf or paperbark and put rocks round it to hold that thing down, so nothing will get in. We got to stay in that cave, and if we run out of meat or anything, all the men go out hunting through the rain. Just get a kangaroo and whatever they could find. And all the wife and the kids in the cave had a big fire going all the time in the doorway, keep it warm. When they come back to the cave, we'll just cook it just there and eat it. They were still doing it when I was a little girl about ten years old, in the 1930s.

Then, if rain stop, we just got to stay there one more days, let the ground get dry properly, then we move out back to the place where we were before. It got pretty muddy, and nice soft ground now, digging all the potatoes. Get a lot now. Some we put on the shelf in the cave, so no one will get it. We used to make a wooden dish and put them all there. When we hungry we know where to go to get them. Put some stores in the cave, and cover it with that paperbark. It stay there, no one would get it, because it's on a shelf, way up. Even little wild onions, in the dish, the old people used to leave them there. When we're really hungry and we couldn't get anything we can go back and we got the food there, see. But we got plenty sweet stuff. Every day they used to get wild honey. They used to fill the little bowl and keep it all the time. Mix it with the water and have a cool drink or something like that. No fridge, no anything. Only just have spears and boomerangs and whatever little wooden dish they make. That's all they used to keep in there.

No clothes, only kangaroo fur and bird feathers they used to get. They used to get the kangaroo tail, pull the strings all clean, and they used to keep him and let him get dry. They keep strings dry; when they want to use it they put it in the water, soak it, make it soft so they can tie something really tight, and then wax, from the spinifex. Use that one like glue for sticking handle and things — that's to do the spears and everything. Or tomahawk; when they're making it, they use that. It's really good, too.

They used to make wool out of their hair, and they used to make a skirt then. We used to do it too, when we was a little girl. They used to give us a stick and teach us to make the wool. Make a big roll first, like that wool that whitefella doing it, but we do it different way. We use our toe to wind it together, make it long. If it's a skirt, we must make it little bit top of the knees, and then cut it after and make a belt. Skirt will be nice. That's the skirt they used to make, and boys only have got a cock-rag thing, just in the front and the back, nothing in the leg side, and the belt. Before all the whitefellas come up, that's the way they used to be. When the whitefellas come up they had jeans and things, then, but usually they used to do bush way, living in the bush all the time. No shirt, just with the skirt. All their skin was just black with the sun burn.

But when I was a girl I never wear that one. I seen them making it, still making it to show the young generation coming up what they used to do in the early days before the whitefella come. When I was born I had a whitefella father, and I had clothes and everything, blanket and things. But they used to still do it when we go to bush meetings; in the bush, they used to still do it. They wear them in the mallalu time — they call it mallalu — the young fella going through the Law. They wear them then, wear that proper belt from the hair, not the whitefella belt. They got to use everything bush way when they putting a boy through the Law.

Early days before the whitefella come, they had a different Law. Say I a woman, when I start getting a period I not allowed anywhere that big mob might be camping. They put that woman with the period separate, one side. She got her own camp. Only the old ladies used to look after, take her food or whatever she want, water or something. That's a secret sort of a thing. No man allowed to go there, or little boys or little girls. She by herself till the period's over, then she come back to the people. She got to be separate. If they moving from there, she got to go one side, and this big mob are going in the one road, and she's got to go hiding all the time till in the next camp. Because those days no clothes — only had the kangaroo skin sort of a thing.

And when she getting a period she got to put a black mark on her face with charcoal. Her husband know then she's getting a period, see. The husband don't do anything, and she move out from the camp, separate, for a few days. Every month, they used to do that. It's very hard, those days, but they know how to work it, themselves. The grannies used to tell me.

Abridged from *Under A Bilari Tree I Born*
Alice Bilari Smith with Anna Vitenbergs and
Loreen Brehaut, 2002

May O'Brien

MY STORY

Mission records state that I was born in the Eastern Goldfields town of Laverton in Western Australia during one of my family's visits to the area. This is incorrect. I was born in the bush and delivered according to Aboriginal tradition, near the mining town of Patricia, Western Australia, where my father (a white man, unknown to me) worked. My birth, like that of many other Aborigines at that time, is not registered.

Australian policy right up to the 1940s stated that all part-Aboriginal children be taken away from their mothers and assimilated into the white community. All children who showed evidence of being part white were caught and transported to Perth. They were institutionalised and trained for domestic and government service.

Since I was classified part-Aboriginal by government

departments of the time, I was placed on their list to be taken away. Police scoured the bush but they could never catch me. At the age of five I was taken by friends who wanted to protect me to Mount Margaret Mission where I spent the next twelve years. Growing up at this place was special. One of the joys was to go to school. This may sound strange but it kept us safe from the hassle of authorities raiding our camps.

As schooling was not compulsory for Aboriginal children, the Education Department had established no schools for us. The Mission chose to provide schools to give us the opportunity to learn as the white children did. There were no qualified teachers at Mount Margaret but the Mission staff did what they could for us. It opened up a new world for me. Many Mission staff received Western Australian Correspondence School lessons for their own children. These were passed on to us, but because there were too many children for full-time lessons we were split into two groups. One group was taught in the morning, the other in the afternoon. Each group got two and a half hours schooling a day. It wasn't much, but for us it was exciting and gave us grounding in all subjects, particularly English. In many schools speaking 'native' was a punishable offence. At Mount Margaret it was different. Teachers encouraged students to speak only English during school hours. They said it was the best way to learn a new language quickly and correctly. Outside school we were able to talk to each other in our own language.

I have only happy memories of my time at Mount Margaret Mission and will always appreciate the background the Missionaries gave me.

Abridged from *Badudu Stories*, teaching notes
May O'Brien and Alwyn Evans, 1994.

Jukuna Mona Chuguna

MY LIFE IN THE DESERT

When I was a child I lived in the sand dune country of the Great Sandy Desert to the south of Fitzroy Crossing. My father's birthplace is near the waterhole called Wirtuka. My father got his name, Kirikarrajarti, right there. It's a name that came from the *ngarrangkarni*. In the ngarrangkarni, two men came to Wirtuka and found the place overrun with possums. They were all fighting and biting each other, some up in the trees and others down in holes in the ground. As they fought they were hissing, 'Kkir! Kkir!' so the two men called the place Kirikarrajarti, because of the hissing noise the possums made. My father's *jarriny* is the possum, and he is called Kirikarrajarti after this place where the possums were fighting.

My mother came from another group of people, who belonged to Japirnka waterhole. When my parents had been together for a while, I was conceived, and my jarriny comes from near the *jila* Mantarta. Near Mantarta is a smooth sandhill called Lantimangu. It's a place where spirit children live. When a husband and wife walk near there, one of the spirits thinks, 'I'll go to them. I'll make them a mother and father.' One time my parents got a lot of edible gum from desert nut trees that were growing all around there, on the flat down from Lantimangu. That night my father had a dream and saw a child standing behind him, but when he turned round it disappeared. Next day he said to his wife, 'This gum might be the jarriny for our baby.' He had a feeling about it. Then my mother knew she was expecting me, and so my spirit comes from that sandhill called Lantimangu.

There was a really bad spirit child living at Lantimangu. He was my spirit brother. He threw a fighting stick at my grandmother and hit her on the back because she was digging up a root vegetable from his place. He snatched the roots from her and left her there on the ground, crippled.

My mother's father also came from the Japirnka waterhole, but his wife, my grandmother, was from Mayililiny waterhole, to the east, near the Canning Stock Route. My grandfather travelled over there and brought her back to be his wife. My father's mother belonged to Tapu and Wayampajarti, two waterholes north of Japirnka.

My mother had four children, three girls and a boy. My father had two other wives besides my mother. His second wife, who was my mother's sister, had three boys and a girl.

My father's third wife had a girl and a boy. All ten of us had the same father.

Our regular journeys for hunting and collecting food took us around the country to the north and to the south of Mantarta waterhole. Although Mantarta is a jila, it hasn't got a water serpent in it.

When I was a child I learnt to kill small lizards to eat. I killed the thorny devil, dragon lizards, and small marsupials. I cooked them myself and ate them. Sometimes my grandmother or older sister would kill a blue-tongue lizard for me.

After the wet season, we'd leave Mantarta and hunt and gather around the freshly watered country. As we travelled we drank water from pools in the swampy ground, then we returned to Mantarta. We hunted and gathered west of Mantarta, getting water from the *jumu* Nyalmiwurtu, Lirrilirriwurtu, Yirrjin, Warntiripajarra and Pirnturr. These were jumu we drank from as we travelled about after the wet season when jumu had water in them.

Our journeys also took us to quite a few jila south of Mantarta — Wirtuka, Paparta, Mukurruwurtu, Warnti and Japirnka.

Some years, in the cold weather, we travelled north to other permanent waterholes. We went to Walypa, then to Wayampajarti, Wirrikarrijarti, Kurralykurraly and to Wanyngurla. At Wanyngurla there were a lot of bush onions to gather and eat. We also went to Tapu, then Kurrjalpartu, Wiliyi and Kayalajarti.

Following the rainy season and right through into the cold season we gathered many different grass seeds to eat. These are the names of the grasses: nyarrjarti, puturu, ngujarna, nyalmi, manyarl, jiningka, purrjaru and karlji. We call this kind of food *puluru*. We also gathered bush onions. Another food we gathered in that season was the nectar from various hakea and grevillea blossoms. We used to suck the nectar from the flowers or soak the flowers in water to make a sweet drink.

When the hot season came, we gathered seeds from acacia trees. We also collected flying termites that we found in antbed. People used to go looking for them in the early morning with a heavy stick, and smash the antbed with the stick to get termites. They used a coolamon to separate some of the termites from the dirt and covered the rest with sand to pick up later. When they came back they uncovered them and separated the rest of them, and then took them back to their camp. They put the termites out in the sun to dry and left them there until they were crisp. Only then were they ready to eat, after the sun had done its work. Everybody ate them — they were delicious.

We used to eat a desert nut called *ngarlka*. The nuts dropped to the ground when they were ripe. The whole year round we could gather them from under the trees, in the hot season and the cold season. We could eat them any time. The new nuts hang there on the trees unripe until the hot season comes.

For food we used to hunt and kill feral cat, bandicoot,

dingo, fox, two kinds of hare-wallaby, sand goanna, different kinds of snake, rough-tailed goanna, blue-tongue lizard and echidna.

We travelled like that year after year, from one waterhole to the next, drinking at jila and drinking at jumu, at rockholes and at claypans, hunting animals and gathering the fruit and seeds of the land.

A good rainy season made the grasses grow well and gave us many kinds of seed and plenty of nectar from the flowers. In a poor wet season, very little grass grew and there wasn't much seed for us to gather. In a good year with a lot of rain we were able to store away the seed to eat later on.

To store the seed we would strip some bark from a paperbark tree to wrap the seed in a parcel, or we'd gather some strong grass and use that to make a container like a nest for holding the seed. We wrapped the seed tightly in packages, and tied them up. Then we cut four forked sticks from a tree, put rails across, and built a frame on top of them. We arranged parcels of food wrapped up in grass or bark on the frame. Then we built a small hut over the top of it to prevent the food from getting dry. We left it there so that we could come and get it later when we needed it and the trees no longer had seeds.

Sometimes we stored seeds, particularly acacia seeds, in a hole in the ground. We used to line the hole with grass, put in a layer of seeds and cover it with bark and then sand. Later, when there was no food left in the bush for us to gather, we came back to get it. We pulled the seeds out of the hole. To get rid of the strong wattle seed smell, we washed them. We cooked them in the fire and then ground them with water till they became a paste, and we ate it like that.

When people went hunting for animals in the hot season, they made sandals for themselves from the bark of the *yakapiri* bush. And that is what they called the sandals, yakapiri. These protected their feet from the burning hot sand. They speared foxes, feral cats, wallabies and sand goannas. The *majirri* has disappeared from the desert now.

Sometimes in the hot season, we'd set off to a waterhole a long way off. We'd set off late in the afternoon, when the day was a little cooler, carrying water in our coolamons. As we walked, we drank the water until there was none left. When it was time to camp for the night, the adults found a claypan that had recently held water. They dug up some of the damp clay and threw it around on the ground to make a cool place for us to sleep. We set off again early in the morning while it was still cool, and went on to the jila.

I'll tell you some more about when I was a child. I was taught to use a coolamon for separating seed from the sand and bits of grass. My grandmother took my hands and held them under the coolamon. 'This is the way you separate the seed,' she said, as she showed me how to shake it. She taught me not to jerk the coolamon around, because then the seed wouldn't separate properly. I didn't really master that separating action till a long time later, when I was bigger. By then I could do a good job of separating the seed from the debris.

I learned to cook meat in the same way. I used to kill small animals and bring them home uncooked. My grandmother and I lit the fire, then she said, 'Bring me a *yirnti* and we'll cook the meat. You must leave the meat in the coals until it's well cooked. You can't eat it if it's only half done. You can only eat it if it's cooked properly.'

I also learned to cook ngarlka by moving them around in the fire. When we had raked them about in the coals for a certain length of time, they'd be just right to eat.

Sometimes a mother dog brought back lizards and regurgitated them whole for her puppies. We snatched them from the pups and rolled them in the sand to clean off the slime. Then we cooked them on the fire and ate them.

My grandmother used to tell me about the people with the pink skin, called *kartiya*. I was curious and kept asking her about them. I imagined kartiya were like trees or dogs or something.

'What are kartiya like? Do they look like blood? Or are they like ashes? Tell me.'

She'd answer, 'No, they are like people. They have two eyes, a mouth and a nose. And two hands.'

'Do they have hair?'

'Yes, of course they have hair.'

I had often seen blood. When I killed a small lizard, some of its blood dripped onto my hand or onto the wooden shovel. 'Are kartiya the colour of this blood from the lizard?' I'd ask.

'Yes, just like that.'

I was really curious about these kartiya.

Abridged from *Two Sisters: Ngarta & Jukuna*
Ngarta Jinny Bent, Jukuna Mona Chuguna,
Pat Lowe and Eirlys Richards;
translated from the Walmajarri by Eirlys Richards, 2004.

Joan Winch

MY MOTHER

My mum was an undemanding sort of a person who couldn't say no to people. She used to always do things for others, like washing, cooking and house cleaning. If somebody came to the door who needed her help it was never too much trouble. That's probably the way she was brought up, to go and do things for other people, for white people, you know, because they used to train Aboriginal girls to be domestic servants in those days. Mum was taken away from her family when she was two years old, so I suppose she didn't know any different. When you're that young you don't ask what happened to your mother or your father or even wonder how your life is going to turn out.

So Mum was bought up by people who weren't her family. When she was fourteen, she was farmed out from Moore River Settlement to a place called Petworth Park in Moora, where she worked as a farm girl. I have some photos of her sitting there on the farm. She was a nanny to the kids and also helped with the cooking. That was the fate of many young Aboriginal girls and that was the kind of work she did on and off till the day she died.

Mum was a wonderful mother. She was very good with her hands and great at making jams and cakes. Every time we had the school fete they would send down and ask her to make a cake to raffle. On rainy days she'd entertain me by making little dolls out of stockings — we didn't have any money to buy toys. She also showed me and my two brothers how to paint; she was a great artist herself. She knitted our clothes and she taught me how to knit and crochet and I was quite good at it. Since I was the only girl in the family, she liked to teach me homemaking things so we were real cobbers.

When I was young I didn't know where Mum came from or who her people were. Mum didn't know herself, but my dad was a Nyungar man. He was Phillip Heath from Katanning, and he was the one who kept us three kids in line.

The Chief Protector of Aborigines, A.O. Neville, had been very angry when Mum married Dad, because at that time a woman was supposed to marry someone lighter in colour than she was. The Aborigines Department was trying to breed out our colour so we wouldn't exist anymore. That's what White Australia was all about. Probably Neville was angry too because Mum had worked for him as a housegirl then gone and married someone he wouldn't approve of behind his back. The Native Welfare controlled every aspect of your life in those days. It was very hard for Aboriginal people then and I learned very young that I'd have to be determined if I wanted to get anywhere.

It's funny the things you learn in childhood. I remember an annual work picnic for Dad's work that we attended once as a family, I learned a valuable lesson there. I was a fast runner so I entered the open race and won. I was really excited and ran over to my parents, shouting, 'I won! I won!' I couldn't believe it! The prize was an electroplated nickel sugar bowl, which was a big thing in those days. The next thing though — they were running the race again. Well, that was it! I wasn't going to be beaten by anyone, so I lined up again and I won again, only this time by an even bigger margin. I've still got that sugar bowl, but nothing before or since has more graphically signified to me the uphill road that we have as Aboriginal people in competing in Australian society.

I loved my mother very much, but I lost her when I was only twelve going on thirteen. With no sisters to talk to I really felt it deeply. It was a terrible blow. She was still with our family in spirit for quite a while though, which wasn't unusual because as Nyungar people we are used to living with spirits. I grew up talking about gennarks and other sorts of spiritual things. After Mum died though, the spiritual world came a lot closer to me.

Not long after she passed away, I was sitting in the

dining room doing some mending when suddenly I felt a bit strange. There was something at the back of my neck and it made me look up. There was Mum, standing in the passageway, as clear as day. Well, I nearly died of shock! My brain told me she was dead, but there she was, standing there. And she wasn't just like a flimsy bit of white smoke that people sometimes describe when they say they've seen a ghost, she was a real person. I didn't know what to do, so I rushed outside, jumped on my pushbike and started riding, all the time thinking, 'I'm not going home because Mum is supposed to be dead.' I rode until around six o'clock at night, it was getting dark by then and I started to worry. If we weren't home by five Dad used to give us the father of a hiding, so I ended up going home.

'Well,' Dad said when he saw me. 'Where were you?'

'Oh Dad don't touch me! I saw Mum and I got a fright and ran out.'

Luckily he understood about spirits so everything was all right. In Dad's family whenever anyone died his dead mother came and knocked on the window to let them know someone close had gone. Every time he saw his mother knock on the window he knew another member of the family had gone, so he understood what had happened to me.

In fact, after Mum died he used to go down to the backyard with a lantern every night after tea to talk to her. When he returned he'd say, 'I've just been talking to your mother and she is worried about you kids because she doesn't think I can look after you.' We would look at him as if he was a bit funny, then we'd go into the bedroom and bounce up and down on the beds and throw pillows at each other and say, 'Dad is going mad, the old man is going mad.'

Then there was our old dog Dale, he was as bad as Dad because he really missed Mum. Our place was one house down from the corner and Dale used to wait up there in the long grass for her to come home from work. The only time he would plod down the road was to get something to eat, then he would plod back up again and sit in this little nest he'd made and wait. So there were the two of them, the dog on the corner waiting for Mum and Dad down the backyard talking to Mum about us kids every evening. This went on for three months, until finally Dad came back one night and said, 'That's it, your mother is gone now. She's happy that I can look after you kids, so now she's gone.' He didn't go down the backyard with the lantern any more and the dog came back from waiting at the corner.

Things settled down then, but there was always a big gap in my life from losing Mum so young. She was only in her early forties when she died. There was another gap too, from not knowing who her people were. Poor old Mum never even knew her family name and she never had the chance to touch base with her people while she was still on this earth. It breaks my heart to think about it, but everything worked out later.

After Mum died I learned to stand alone. I had one older brother and one younger brother and I was expected to take over the complete running of the household. Dad worked at the gasworks and his clothes got very gritty; there was no washing machine so I had to learn in a hurry how to do things well. It was hard, but it stood me in good stead for later life. I learned to be self-reliant and self-disciplined. I learned other things too. With Dad you had to think before you put up any of your ideas, otherwise they'd just be wiped away. So I learned to think a lot and to listen to what others were saying before I spoke up.

One day I was making watery stew when a kid from down the street said to me. 'What are ya doing?'

'Just making stew for tea,' I told him.

'Why don't ya put some flour and water in it to make it thick?'

'Why don't you?' I replied.

So he did. He made a stew and it was just like Mum used to make. I learned a valuable lesson from that. When someone knows what they're talking about, listen.

Abridged from *Speaking from the Heart*
edited by Sally Morgan, Tjalaminu Mia and
Blaze Kwaymullina, 2007.

Lola Young

GROWING UP WITH FAMILY

When I was a young girl my grandparents teach me everything. That's why I know all the bush plants, but they only teach me the important plants, they never teach me about all the other shrubs, only the name and if it has flowers and things like that. They say, 'Don't teach that one, that's just the shrubs, that's just the plant and thing, not good for anything else.'

When I first going with them I used to worry. I was frightened of them because they growl too much. You got to get used to them, nobody else around. Nothing I could do, when Mum and Dad say you staying with the grandparents, you stay, whether you crying or not. You stay! My cousins, sisters and brothers never used to be left with the old grandparents, only me. Mum and Dad say to me, 'You stay. That's where you learn. You stay right here.' If I still want to run and chase Mum and Dad when they leaving, they get off and give me a hiding and send me back. So I couldn't do nothing, I had to learn.

My grandparents reckoned I was the chosen one for them, to learn all these things, because I was the first grandchild. I went through all that, like you go to high school, you know. I never been to school, but they teaching me proper. They got to give you mark for it just like you going to high school. They give me top mark because I know everything about the bush and everything. That's only my knowledge, to learn all them things. I have that special skill.

My name, my Aborigine name, is Ngamingu; I was born at Rocklea Station, in the station just at the back, on 12 February 1942. I was the first child. Then was Nicholas, my sister Doris (Minga) and Colin. My dad passed away after that and Mum remarried. Then she had Kevin, Brian and Aquinas. Nicholas and Doris were born at Cobor, outstation from Rocklea, Colin was born on Kooline Station. Kevin, Brian and Aquinas were born in Onslow Hospital.

My dad's name was Cookie; Cook, they called him. His Aborigine name is Kurubungu. He was born in Hamersley Station. My son Rodney named after him now. My mum's name is Dora. Her Aborigine name is Mithakunti; she was born in Mithakunti – Sandy Creek, they call it. My mother and my grandparents are from Rocklea. My stepdad's name is Dan, Danny Gilba.

Mum was Kurrama, my dad Panyjima, and I follow

the Yinawangka way. I never followed the two parents; I followed the grandfather, Yinawangka. I don't know how that comes about. I was the oldest and the grandparents teach me all the culture things and I have to follow my grandparents. My grandmother was Kurrama. I should have followed the grandmother, but too late now. I speak a mixture of Panyjima and Kurrama, but not Yinawangka. We never used to speak Yinawangka and now Yinawangka is nearly all gone.

Some of my growing up was on Rocklea Station and some on Juna Downs Station. We was up and down to Juna Downs, because my father was a horse breaker and he used to break in horses on every station. Juna Downs was the place he used to stay most of the time; just come back to Rocklea to visit all the family, my grandmothers and everyone. We used to come visit only on the holiday; in those days they call holidays pink eye. We travel by horse, horseback riding, or sometimes in a cart, horse and cart. Those days they used to have their own horses, packhorses.

Good life, growing up in the bush – free, nice and wild. Horseback riding all the time. We had no cars anyway; they only had few cars around those days. Dad taught us how to ride. Falling off the horse, that's nothing. Get on again, because we have to – Dad tell us to get on again. We used to go riding all the time when there was two of us. Brother Nick would ride with Dad and I used to ride behind Mum on her horse. We used to go everywhere. Take a packhorse, go dogging in the back country, catch a fish, whatever you want. A good free life.

When Mum start having the other one – sister we lost now, Doris – we never used to go anywhere any more. Dad reckoned three is too many to go around everywhere. He left Mum and us in Cobor with Auntie Alice and Uncle Jack Smith while he went dogging and working on the stations nearby.

We went down to Mulga Downs Station with Dad and all the old people there used to give us some dry bread, save it for us in a white bag. No time to cook when we moving, just chew on that dry bread, or soak him in the tea to soften him up.

Sometimes when we were camping, Mum used to make some Johnny cakes. Is like a damper, just cook it on top on the coals. You mix it like a damper, but is a quick one. You just chuck it on the coals and turn him over again. All on top.

No sweets; we don't know sweets, don't know lollies. Only time we have a lolly was when we come back to Rocklea with Dad, maybe come back to do some breaking in horses or come in for the rations. The station owner, Walter Smith, every time he see us coming he used to line us up and ask who want a lolly. He had them big long hard-boiled lollies you used to get in the old days, all colours. You got to hit it with a rock, break it. Brother Nick and cousin what we lost, Des Smith, we used to fight over it, and Des used to say, 'Well we got to share it.' He'd go and get a rock and break it all up and give us little bit each.

We used to be on the move all the time, but when we in Juna Downs we set – good, you know, time to play around. We never used to have toys, nothing to play with, just us, play one with other one. We used to play around with big horses. Dad used to break them in quiet for us. If Mum and Dad sleeping it off after dinner we used to get on that horse and go. We jump on him bareback, no bridle, because that horse was so quiet. We used to pull his mane down when we want him to come down, then jump all over him. He was a very old white horse, a mare, call him Ladybird. Doesn't matter that we small; we used to jump on that horse to go around hunting, go around gathering the bush tucker, get all the wild fruits and things, then come back.

We used to bring a live lizard back and chuck it on Mum when she was asleep. She used to scream and chase us away. We were really good with a rock to get a goanna or anything. Hit him on the head, cook him. Come back and surprise Mum and Dad, tell them, 'We got something to eat.'

They used to ask us, 'Where you fellas got that?'

'Out there in the bush, where else?'

We never know to talk English then, we used to talk our own language.

When I was an early age we got back to Rocklea and Dad went to one of the stations. He was getting sick then. He had ulcers in his stomach and every camp we used to go he used to dig a little hole and spit blood into that hole. One time he got up and got really angry with himself and we went and get this bush medicine, *yajiri* (native mustard).

Boil that up in the pot and drink it while it's hot. Just how you drinking hot tea, just enough to be drinkable, drink it down while it's hot. That fix him right up, finish, never spat blood again.

Long way after, we all moved down to Onslow because Dad was getting sicker. We stayed in town, where Bindi Bindi is now, in a tent. No house there then, just a little bush and a big tree. There was a little well there for water, not far from the hospital. Everybody used to come in there, washing and everything. Put a bucket down with a rope, get the water.

Dad went to Port Hedland Hospital on the doctor plane and Mum didn't know what to do. My sister was just a baby, sitting up, and Mum thought, Oh well, no one going to feed us. She sat down and talked to us kids: 'We got no more Dad here – we have to earn our own living now.' It was hard because we used to the bush, we not used to living in town. No Aborigine people were there when we went down to Onslow. Dad had a couple of Malay friends, the Ahmats; they used to run the bakery there. I worked in the bakery. I might have been about ten years old. Not used to living in town and didn't know work, you know.

Mrs Ahmat give me a job greasing the bread tins and sweeping out the bakery and watering all the trees. Nick was little bit smaller than me and he went to work in the butcher shop. He used to go out with old Jack Whittaker the butcher man, shaking along the road in the little sulky. His job was cleaning the blocks, so he could bring some meat home for us. I used to bring home bread, Nick some meat. Didn't get wages; they give me bread and clothing. Mrs Ahmat used to sew some clothes for me – silky, with puffed up sleeves and tie a belt behind. We don't know what nice clothes is, because in the old days we only used to have those little things like a little strap coming down in front. Mum would find a job cleaning the house for white ladies, washing and ironing and things. She worked that way. My sister would go with her, sit out on the verandah waiting for Mum to finish work; if she tired, Mum would put her to sleep.

We stayed in Onslow about four or five months and my uncle, Jack Smith, come then. He know his brother gone to Port Hedland. I think Dad got in touch with him somehow and told him to go and look for the family belong to him. Jack Smith was a kangaroo shooter then, all around Rocklea and Cobor. He come down to Onslow there and he was buying a new truck, ordered a Morris truck coming in the boat. Come down there and pick us up then.

He find a job for Mum in Ashburton Downs Station. Mum was cooking there; she was a good cook. Me and Nick had to work at the station, and that's where we really, really learnt to work. It was tougher than where we start in Onslow. Nick used to work in the yard gardening, like a yardman, watering lawn and everything. That station had a lot of dogs and he used to take all the dogs for a walk. Old lady on the station had ten dogs in a kennel.

That old lady, white lady, used to be really rough. Her name was Olga, Mrs Kelly. Used to grab us, whip us in the corner with them little bamboo sticks. Used to whip me if I'm not doing any job, or if I don't listen sometimes. I lived in the station because I had to get up early, and not far for me to get up, have a shower and go to work; just there. I had a room, toilet, bathroom, like a little cottage. Sometimes my grandmother sleep there with me, when she want to. Mum used to come to work early from their camp not far away.

I was in the station more than the other kids and sometimes I get carried away and want to talk and play with these kids, my mates. They singing out, 'We going down the creek swimming', or something like that. I can't do that, I have to stay and work. Only on a Sunday I used to go. Lot of those old people that are here now, my aunties, they never used to work. I used to say to other young girls going along, 'Why me, only me?' Other young girls used to come and tell Mum they want a dinner; they cut the lunch, get a drink and everything, then go down the creek swimming all day. I used to hate it, I want to go too, but I can't – must stay and work.

I was the one with the little white cap on and big white apron and them big long dresses. You got to have shoes on all the time, got to be clean to come to work. I was the house girl cleaning and polishing the wooden floor. You got to go down on your knees – no mop those days. You got to shine it up and nearly see your face in it. If you don't do that, you got to go back and do it again. Old white woman used to give us a hiding if we don't do the job. Scrub it first, then run the polish over, then rub the polish off. Really hard! My knee used to be finished. Had to clean the silver, set the table up and things like that. Got to be spotless for that woman.

I'm the one used to wait on them when they having a feed. I used to sit in the corner waiting on the people eating. You know when the whitefellas have a dinner they have the soup first, so I bring the soup in, then get the tray and get all the dishes when they finish, take them to the kitchen. Then bring the dinner and sit down waiting in the corner until they finish. That was really, really hard, and I was learning a lot of different things all the time. I had to do all those things.

Mr and Mrs Kelly changed the old ways the Aborigine people lived at the station. We had to know how to dress, keep clean and eat at the table. They teach us to eat at the table. They change the house and all, made a big dining room thing for the blackfellas, no more having our meals in the woodheap, like the other stations. That's why, sort of, they change our lives, you know.

Had to keep clean and know how to dress and things like that. In early days old people never used to have pants and them things. That lady now used to order all the clothes: pants and petticoats, bras and everything. Old people used to say, 'I feel uncomfortable with this cockrag on.' They used to call pants a cockrag.

We used to have fun dressing the old girls, laugh and everything. We have a good laugh when we put that bra on Auntie Mabel and them. They say, 'What this! Is too tight, hurting my *piwi* and everything.' They have the biggest laugh about it. Mrs Kelly tell them, 'You have to wear them, this is different now. Grab all the old clothes and chuck them in the bin.' Then she make them old people wear them things, petticoat, pants and bra, and she come with a bamboo stick, lift their dress up when they not looking, you know, checking if they got pants on. They say, 'Aah, what all having a look at my *thumpu'* [backside], and all that. They used to get shame, yeah. She used to be really strict, check it if they got pants on, because when they get home they chuck it away, feel free again.

All the old people, when they get the calico material, used to sew pants and things for us little kids, but they never used to have it, you know. 'I don't know why that woman maybe worrying about our *thumpu* – we born with nothing', they say, you know. The other old girls used to them things, Mum and them. Them hard corset thing, they used to put it on Mum, because my Mum was big, put the stomach down, you know. When they have a party or something, I used to put my foot on Mum's tummy and push it back and somebody used to lace that thing straight away, you know, lace it up zigzag and tie him up. We used to have the biggest laugh. 'Walk straight,' they tell us. We had some fun all right.

Dad got better and worked at Munda Station. He never come back. The doctor in Port Hedland was trying him out, keeping an eye on him, Munda not far from Port Hedland Hospital, you know. Anyway, we stayed at Ashburton Downs. Long time later, Dad died, but I don't remember when that was.

No men around, so me and my brother used to go and kill a sheep for the station. It's no trouble for us to ride a horse to go get one, we already know them things. You got to go out and get the sheep, bring them in and put them in the yard, then put them in the pen when they settle down. Whenever you want to kill them, kill them. Mum's brother, Stanley Delaporte, he used to teach us how to grab them and how to sit on them and all that. Lucky we learning as we going. We had to learn tough ways, that's the only way to learn how to work.

We used to grab him, cut his throat. I'm the one used to cut the throat. Sound like a murderer! Boy, did we make a mess of that sheep, skinning it. We had to skin it rough ways at first, not properly; then you got really used to it, you know. You got to learn how to do it. We had to put it up on a hook and it used to drop down on the ground. Try to put it up again with Nick down the back trying to put the weight on the pole to lift it up. We used to sing out for one old fellow, one old grandfather. He used to come and help us. Then get the sheep down and cut him up in the meat house.

Anyway, I worked there, and this Mission time coming up now. Mum took Nick and my sister to Carnarvon Mission to go to school then. They never sent them to Onslow, sent them straight to the Mission. Mum come back to work again, leave those two in the Mission, and the Inspector, Mr Geer, come look for me then. Asked Mum, 'You got another older daughter somewhere?' They had it in the paper, they was looking for me. Mum said, 'Yes.' Dobbed me in!

That white woman, Mrs Kelly, she didn't want me to go; she hide me away, tell me to go bush till the Inspector go away. She used to tell me, 'Inspector coming looking for you, to take you to school. You got to saddle up your horse and go.' We sit down and watch from the hill, seen the stranger car coming, dust coming, you know. Soon as he's coming closer, I gone. I'd saddle the horse up and go down the creek, hiding. Stop all day while the Inspector there looking for all the kids. I didn't want to go.

If something different going to happen to you, might be Inspectors and things like that, you be touchy – what going to come at you next time? I was thinking that bush life was good in the early days, but when we first moved into Onslow all these different things happen, and job getting more and more tougher as we grew. I didn't know what was going to happen to me if they sent me to the Mission. That woman said, 'Oh, she not here.' She used to cover for me as I'm the last one to work there. Anyway, they went away, didn't find me. I stayed at the station. I was fourteen then. Been long time there now, working.

Abridged from *Lola Young: Medicine Woman and Teacher*
Lola Young with Anna Vitenbergs, 2007.

David Simmons

HIDING

I was born in Subiaco, Perth. My mother is an Aboriginal woman from Kukerin in the Lake Grace area of Western Australia. My father came from the Margaret River area. He is an Aboriginal man. My stepfather is part of the Isaacs family from Perth. My parents are Nyoongahs.

My schooling as a young fella was undertaken at different places. Our family used to travel around a lot then.

In 1951 the Native Welfare Officers were still active. My younger school days were occasionally spent hiding from the Native Welfare. My mother insisted that I go to school, but there was always that dread that I would never come home from school because of Native Welfare. We knew that if Native Welfare ever found out that there were Aboriginal kids like myself at those schools, they would take them away. Native Welfare didn't necessarily go and tell the parents that they had taken their child. We were all vulnerable to Native Welfare, who were always grabbing Aboriginal kids. I started school in 1950. I would turn six in June so I had to start when I was five and a half years old. It was at a very small place called Parkerville. I've been back since, taken my kids, it's just a one-room building.

Parkerville is up in the Darling Ranges, not far from Mundaring. We shifted there as the old man, my stepfather, was a returned soldier working at Hollywood Repatriation Hospital in Perth. Some of the old returned soldiers had country properties. He used to negotiate with them. The family had to keep out of the way of the Native Welfare because Mum wouldn't give up her Aboriginality.

Not long after I started school we shifted to Mount Helena. It is another very small place back in the hills around Perth. I used to catch the bus to school myself. The school building there was the town hall. Quite a few kids went to the town hall. There was more than two busloads, all mixed up, but I was probably the only Aboriginal kid at school. I can remember my mother taking me to school and asking the teacher, if the Native Welfare were to come, would they hide me?

I remember that on several occasions that a Scottish teacher called Miss Lang raced into the class and grabbed me saying, 'Quick, quick, come in here.' And she got another boy, who is my friend to this day, to go with me and hide under the wooden stage. So we ran and hid under the stage. She said, 'Don't you kids come out until I tell you.' The Native Welfare man came in and asked if there were any Aboriginal children at school and the teacher said, 'No.' It was probably an hour or so before we could come out.

On another occasion we were out in the yard playing when the Native Welfare officer came. She told one of the kids to get me and go up under the hall. We had to climb right under the school. A few of the kids came with us and they thought it exciting hiding under the school until the Native Welfare bloke went. But it wasn't a prank for me. I think these visits were a response to someone dobbing me in, but I'm not sure.

But we were dobbed in on a couple of occasions when we were at Parkerville because the bloke came to our house. But we had a system. Mum set it up. There was a tree two hundred metres away from the house and another about five hundred metres away. She would leave bottles of water under the trees. The system was that if the Native Welfare came we were to rush to the first tree and stay there. The dog was to come with us and he wouldn't let anybody come near without barking a warning. If the dog barked a warning and it wasn't Mum yelling out, then we would go to the next tree which was further out and hide there. We had about half a dozen bottles of water that we would take with us and Mum would give us some bread or damper, whatever she had, and we were off. I was the eldest. We all had fair skin. Clarrie has got the darkest skin of all of us.

Native Welfare would have just grabbed us. My elder brother and sister were in Sister Kate's children's home. Mum put them in Sister Kate's so she knew where they were. In this way she could stop Native Welfare efforts to grab kids. She put Alice and Bill, who are older than me, into Sister Kate's. Sister Kate's at the time had a lot of half caste kids.

Unfortunately Native Welfare took the kids from the south and sent them north. They took kids from the north and brought them south. They crossed the people up all the time.

Mum always taught us about little things when we were kids in the bush. How to track rabbits, know the difference between the animals, how to catch the animals, where to look for them all and which animals we could eat, those sorts of things. The old man worked at Hollywood Repatriation Hospital. He only came home four days in a month. He didn't have a vehicle to drive home every weekend. We wouldn't see the old man for months at a time. What he would do is try to work for three months and then get twelve days off. In this way he had some sort of time off especially when we were on holidays.

So we spent a lot of time at home with Mum. It was really good. She always taught us to respect our elders, which I always follow. When we moved to East Perth we were among a lot of Aboriginal people who were like fringe dwellers. We never turned the people away and we were never afraid to mix with them. I certainly was never afraid of the people. Those were the things that my mother passed on.

Then there was the Coolbaroo League, it means black and white magpie. Back in '55, '56 it had a little meeting place in Murray Street. It was the Young Men's Christian Association, I think. They had a lot of the old people come in there and sit down and tell us stories. In those days they still brought in the traditional spears and shields and boomerangs to those meetings. They used to have a lot of arts and crafts there to sell. Not so much art but craft. We heard all the stories about why the crow was black, how the red robin got red, how the emu and the goannas swapped feathers and all of those stories.

I was never part of a corroboree, never went to one in those days. But there was an elder, Bill Bodney. He was the old tribal top man back in the 1950s, responsible for Perth. I remember to this day when the Queen came, she had to be given the boomerang of peace by old Bill to say that she could come to his country, because that was his place. He was on the airstrip when she came to Australia.

I finished my primary school in East Perth and I went on to high school. It was for boys and I left halfway through the second year, as soon as I turned fourteen. In those days you were allowed to leave school at fourteen. I could have gone on to do wonderful things. I was told by the headmaster that I would have made an excellent accountant. But in those days, you had to know somebody who could get you into accountancy. We didn't have those sorts of contacts.

In those days there was plenty of work around for young blokes straight out of school. I started off working with my brother in a timber mill just up the road from us in Charles Street. The Tower Hotel was on the corner. The old fella next door had a little bit of a timber yard at the back and I worked there for about a year and a half. Then I left and went and worked for an old fella in a nursery.

At this time we'd moved to West Perth. I left school in 1959. We were there for only a short while and got our first State Housing house in Barney Street, Glendalough. Later, I was the last member of the family to live in that house. We lived there until 1986.

Once we were in that house in West Perth, Mum set it up as a halfway house for the kids coming out of Sister Kate's. There was a need which she saw. Kids coming out of Sister Kate's had nowhere to go when they turned fourteen or they finished high school, because then they had to get out.

Not far from us, on the corner of Fitzgerald and Carr Streets, was a place called McDonald House. McDonald House is part of the Aboriginal history. They taught the kids, in a TAFE type situation, to do things like bookkeeping, accounting, etc. It was the first sort of Aboriginal access in Perth. There were limited numbers of kids getting places there, so Mum set up this halfway house. No government funding, just did it off her own bat. The kids who wanted to get into there came and stayed at our place. We had a big four-bedroom house. Mum put beds in, about four or five kids in each room like a little dormitory set up.

They stayed with us. There was plenty of work around so they were able to support themselves and they had a place to come home to, three meals a day or prepared lunches. Then as places became available in McDonald House they went there and they were able to go on with schooling. That worked really well. Mum certainly made use of her time.

Abridged from *Karijini Mirlimirli*
edited by Noel Olive, 1997.

Eric Hedley Hayward
OPPORTUNITY

At the beginning of the 1950s, in line with the changes in government attitude and legislation about social programs for Aborigines, a scheme had been introduced so Noongar students could go to high school in Perth.

How it worked was that officers of the Native Welfare Department identified boys and girls capable of taking up the opportunity, and after a selection process involving the officers, teachers and parents, a committee in Perth made the final selection. Those who were doing well at school and were willing to leave their families were selected first.

This was a great opportunity for Noongars. At that time, living conditions, school costs and the general marginalisation Noongars experienced in the country were factors, we believed, that made it almost impossible to be successful in regional high schools. Few Noongars in the country were achieving results comparable to Wadjalas', and this new opportunity gave us a chance to do so. So, many Noongars thought the idea of kids going away to better themselves was a good one, and, certainly, parents knew they would never have been able to pay for what was on offer from the Native Welfare Department.

But some parents wouldn't allow their children to be sent away. Our communities had experienced many years of forced child removals, and even then children were still being removed from their parents, and so much doubt remained that the program was 'for their own good' rather than just another way to take their kids.

Grandfather Williams had had plenty of experience of Noongars being taken away, and my mother talked to him about allowing kids and teenagers to go away for work or school.

She remembered: 'He was visiting one time and since we began to hear about this education thing for our kids going to high school away in Perth, we talked about it. I wasn't sure about sending my kids away, but I knew deep down that we had to do something to help our kids do better at school. "Wadjalas," he said, "aren't to be trusted with our young ones. Too many have been taken away. Be careful Lily," he told me, "they may never come back. We don't want to lose any more of our people."

Mum understood what he meant. She, too, had almost been taken away by the Protector of Aborigines, and had some reservations about whether going away for schooling would turn out good for her kids and for the family. Uncle Len and Aunty Elsie had their doubts, too. Years before, when their son Jack had been a little boy on the Gnowangerup reserve, he was fearful of being taken away by the authorities. Jack had a fair complexion and was a target for the officers. At the first inkling that the van to take them away was in town, all the fair Noongar kids would run away to the bush and hide. Jack was as scared as hell of being taken away and was one of the first to head for the bush.

Mum said he used to say: 'Why am I so fair? Why do they want to take us fair kids? We are all the one family.'

That stuck with me. I was fair too and could understand how Jack probably felt about being chased down to be taken away. They nearly got away with taking me, so what happened with Jack I never forgot.

It wasn't forgotten by the Williams family either. Like Mum, they had reasons to be reluctant to let their kids go in case they didn't come back. But more Noongars began to believe it was okay and a good thing for their young ones, as some kids went for work or schooling and came back.

In the very early days, many of our women were domestics on sheep stations and farming properties, and then Mum and her mates did that type of work at Gnowangerup. Then younger ones in our families continued similar work. At least six close relations went to properties in the south-west part of Noongar country to work as domestics. Vernice, Dawn and Barbara Williams worked for Egerton-Warburtons in the South-West, and my sisters Norma and Edna worked for Hesters and Muirs there as well. These property owners were among the early settlers of the South-West. Then a lot of young women got work at the Homes of Peace, in Subiaco, as nursing assistants. My sisters Joan, Norma and Wilma worked there, and so did cousins Vernice, Dawn, Barbara, Judy, Treacy, Averil and Rhona. Several of Aunty Elsie's daughters went to Alvan House and on to Homes of Good Peace to work in nursing. As it became apparent they could return home as they wished, our families became more confident in allowing their young ones to venture out on their own.

Not that I lacked confidence about returning. Mum certainly encouraged me, and I knew that Ted Penny, Uncle Bill's stepson, had been in the first group to go to McDonald House, and my brother Bevan attended the following year. And Norma had gone and returned too.

It wasn't as a result of my mother's own schooling that she emphasised the value of education to us — she had never been to school. But she did observe others well and could see the potential in her kids, and of course she knew, as I did from an early age, that Noongars most often got the rough end of the stick in dealings and opportunities in our town and an education was the way this might be changed.

So in February 1960, I got on the train, travelled through the night to Perth, was picked up by Miss Styles, the hostel manager, at the Perth Railway Station and was taken to McDonald House. I had made it. I knew then it was up to me to do the best I could to survive in a new environment — to me, it was a new world.

Living in the city was nothing like I had experienced before. McDonald House was in West Perth, about three kilometres from central Perth, in an old semi-industrial area. The house was above average size and big enough to accommodate a manager, a maid and eight boys. I shared a room with two other boys and had my own bed and a small wardrobe. There was plenty of space. I had come out of a crammed, uncomfortable shack and I thought this was perfect. Three other boys were in a second bedroom, so there were six of us who stayed there for that year.

Most of the boys in the hostel had lived in humpies on reserves, and so it was totally new to live in a spick-and-span home where we were regimented by rules and regulations most of the time. You were told to keep the noise down and be respectful to those in charge. Things were totally different from back home, and learning to be different was hard. But I think that with all the requirements and standards of conduct set for us, we did manage it quite well, considering.

Native Welfare provided us with a set of school, home and social clothes at the beginning of the year, along with football gear and shoes. Generally, clothes and shoes were handed down from one boy to another, though we did get some new clothes at times.

Native Welfare also provided us with five shillings a

week pocket-money for our own use, which seemed like a fortune to us.

The daily routine at the hostel was to get up at seven, make our beds and have a shower. Those on breakfast duty would set the table, make the toast and cook the eggs or whatever we were going to eat, with the help of the maid, Miss Chadd. She was a Noongar lady from Roelands Mission who helped the manager, Miss Styles, run the place. Miss Styles had worked at the mission too. She was a tall and large imposing person who didn't move very quickly but was very aware of how we behaved and made it clear that 'rules were rules' and we had to stick to them, always. I soon learned that we didn't mess with Miss Styles, but still managed to have problems sticking to the rules.

Following breakfast, two others would wash, wipe and put away the dishes. The other two would sweep the floors and tidy the dining room.

Miss Chadd did the washing on Wednesdays. The boys were required to fold and iron their own clothes, and wash their socks, singlets and undies on that day. Every Saturday morning we cleaned and tidied our rooms and washed and polished the floors.

Jobs had to be done properly. Miss Styles insisted the house was always clean, dusted and polished. We had an electric polisher that was big and very difficult to handle and it took a while for the boys to learn to use it safely.

When us new boys first arrived and had our duties

allocated, I recall the older boys from the year before setting us up for the demon polisher. It had a round disc-shape brush that protruded out the front a little, and there were two small wheels at the back that allowed you to move it from one room to another. The motor, which sat on top, turned the single brush in a clockwise direction. When you were polishing, the brush was the only thing that touched the floor. It spun around very fast. Of course new boys didn't know that, not having seen an electric polisher before, let alone used one. The trick was to balance this powerful machine, and if you didn't, it would run off in the direction it was leaning towards, even if you had a firm hold on it. It was difficult to get it right. If it took off it would smash into whatever was in its path. It must have weighed fifteen kilos. It also tended to go off in different directions as you tried to get the balance correct.

There was no instruction from Eddie, an older boy whose job it was to get me going. With him, it was just trial and error. He was a practical joker and had fun watching others mess up. I had to polish the lounge and passage.

'There you go,' he said, after he had pulled the polisher out of the passage cupboard and into the lounge room. 'Switch it on at the switch,' he instructed, as he pointed towards to the switch on the handle.

I had no idea what was to come. I turned the switch on and off it went, whizzing and spinning. I clung to it as that's what Eddie had advised. I hung on in desperation as it went all over the polished boards of the lounge room as

I tried to balance it. Left, right, front and back, the thing went.

'Keep it up level — level — level!' Eddie instructed.

I had no chance of controlling it and all Eddie did was stand behind me to make sure he wasn't run over himself, watch me, laugh his head off and give a few instructions as I battled the demon. It eventually slammed into the wall with me sprawled on the floor but still attached to it.

Eddie quickly switched it off. 'You're done for now.'

At that moment the other older boys poked their heads around the open door, splitting their sides with laughter.

'He's wrecked the house,' one of them yelled. It put a chill up my spine because I didn't want to be sent home.

'Now he's in for it.'

And that made it worse.

I gingerly got up, not knowing whether to have a crack at Eddie or what.

A clump of plaster had been knocked out of the wall but nothing else was damaged. It was the first week of my stay at McDonald House and I didn't have any idea of what I should do about it.

I did tell Miss Styles and fortunately didn't lose any pocket-money on that occasion.

Eventually I did learn to use that polisher, as the other two new boys, Morgan Williams and Morrie Millar, did, and became quite good at it.

Morgan and Morrie soon became the two boys I most associated with; the fact that they came from my area — the central and lower Great Southern — was enough to make us a team and helped me adapt to my new life a great deal.

Saturdays were sport days. We all played footy in winter and went swimming at the beach in summer. Saturday afternoons were for going to watch the league football, when not playing sport ourselves, or socialising. Saturday nights were set aside to go to the movies in one of the Perth theatres.

Sundays were for church-related activities. The morning sessions were held at the North Perth Baptist church and the evenings at the People's Church in Perth, or elsewhere. We also attended the church youth club in North Perth on Friday evenings. At Easter we attended Christian conventions at Brookton.

Each boy in first or second year high school was required to study after school for one and a half hours, four evenings a week. Those in third or higher years studied for two hours.

Adapting to this new life wasn't easy for any of us that year, especially for Morrie, Morgan and me. We came from different environments where we'd developed our own set of rules about behaviour.

Of the six boys from the South-West in my first year in Perth, five of us went to Tuart Hill Senior High and one to Mount Lawley Senior High.

Those of us in our first year were in for another big shock, because we had to fit in pretty quickly with the educational system. At that time, no-one ever considered matters like preparing us for school, the relevancy of course materials and culturally appropriate teaching. Somehow, we just had to cope as best we could. We were receiving a special opportunity.

For me it was the opportunity I'd been waiting for: to continue my education. I knew it was the only way I'd be able to go on to a good education and job. I'd become aware of my own capabilities during my primary schooling and knew I could cope with schooling. I knew I had the ability to do as well as Wadjala kids — in fact, I'd outdone them in several subjects in primary school; one year I even won a biro as a special prize at the Broomehill Anglican Spring Fair for being the neatest and best writer for my age group.

So I knew I was very lucky to get the chance of a high school education. For us Noongar kids, this sort of privilege had an impact on our lives, changing our hopes and aspirations in ways which were just not possible for many others from our communities. At school we dressed the same as everyone else, we carried the same school bags and had all the textbooks and study equipment we needed. Back home it had been considerably different.

The hostel students had lots of friends at school and at Tuart Hill Senior High, students chose three of us five hostel kids to be prefects. Four joined the army cadets. In addition we had opportunities to meet people, visit places and go to events. Once we toured the passenger liner *Oranje*, which was berthed at Fremantle. I also remember going to meetings of the Aboriginal Progress Association, in Bassendean. It was then, too, that I heard about the Coolbarroo League, an organisation run by and for Noongars. It held dances in Perth and several of us Noongar boys from the hostel went to them. All these experiences were good for our social development, and we began to expect a better deal in life.

Abridged from *No Free Kicks*
Eric Hedley Hayward, 2006.

Rene Powell

MISSION DAYS

How does a little Aboriginal kid, who doesn't understand English, somehow drop everything from her early life? No words can describe the feeling of being grabbed from a mother and planted among strangers. I don't remember, but I think I must have been shocked and frightened. I was taken from the most natural childhood imaginable to a very disciplined, strict and boring existence. I daydreamed my way through school. I hated school. Some kids loved learning but I wasn't one of those kids. Like my cousin Molly Cameron — she chose to go there, she went out at Christmas, and she was eight when she went there. Recently Molly said that she remembered the time I first arrived at Mount Margaret.

It was night-time and this little girl walked in and we was saying, 'Who's that little girl? What's her name?'

'Oh, she's from Warburton, she's a little "half-caste" girl from Warburton and her name's Rene.'

She was a little thin one with a big pink woolly jumper — cardigan — on her. Thin little legs. She was head down standing because a big mob of kids was right round her. Yeah — she was frightened to see us. That's how she came into the Home ... I didn't know she was my relation until I went out of the Home.

I didn't choose to go there. I hated it. It was very hard when you were four years old at Mount Margaret. I was all confused. And all these other kids, they were probably in the same boat — never experienced their own little childhood — in this institution where there's a new language and all these rules and Christian songs and stories. And they're alien. So it's hard to learn because you speak and think Aboriginal and then you are thrown into school and you've got to be an expert on ABC.

Every December when school closed the mothers who were not living at Mount Margaret would come to the mission to take their children for the school holidays. Teatime at Mount Margaret Mission was about four or five o'clock. Straight after tea the girls would be locked in the dormitory. Some of the big girls would stand on the beds to look out the windows to see whose mother was coming with a piece of paper in her hand with the child or children's name on it. Everyone would get excited hoping their mother would be seen crossing the creek walking to the girls' home. Soon the dormitory would be silent with the sad and broken-hearted girls whose mothers didn't come. We didn't know it at the time, but only the 'full-blood' girls were allowed to leave the mission with their mothers. 'Half-caste' girls were never given permission to go. I wonder now how the mothers felt when they arrived and were told they couldn't take their children for the holidays. Every second year we would be taken by the mission to Cosmo Newbery or Esperance for the Christmas holidays.

At times, lots of Aboriginal ladies would come there and stand outside the fence near the dormitory yard. My mum could have been standing out there, but after years went by I didn't know her and the other kids wouldn't know her because they were from Mount Margaret. I don't know if I ever saw her then, outside the fence.

During school recess and after school we played games like marbles, jack-bones, skipping, string games and hopscotch until we lost interest in them. One thing that we had all year was the story lead or story wire, a piece of wire we would get from a broken fence and pass around. You sat on the ground and told yourself stories or you took it in turns with a couple of others or in a group. One of the most popular stories was Guess Whose Family? We'd draw the mother, father and their kids. If there were two wives, we drew beds for the first wife and the second wife. You had to guess the family and if you couldn't the storyteller would give clues, the initials of the people or where they came from. The older kids passed it down. That's how we knew who we were. That's how we kept our family history going. The older girls or Aboriginal people at the mission would tell you what they knew about your family, or where you came from, using the story wire. The kids used the story wires for weapons, too. There were lots of fights with kids stealing these story wires.

Kids can be cruel, too. If we had fights they'd call out the names of other kids' mothers and fathers to hurt them or unsettle them or they'd say to me, 'Go back to Warburton, you've got no mother here.' That's how I knew I came from Warburton, but I didn't know where it was.

Lots of girls ran away from Mount Margaret Mission and when they were brought back they were punished. They would get a belting, with a cane or a leather belt. I ran away once — there were about seven of us. Three girls ran away to Laverton the day before us. They took off after breakfast and three of us took off really early the next day. We hadn't gone far when we heard these other girls behind us shouting. They were younger girls and we tried to make them go back. But they wouldn't go, so we said, 'Come along. You can come with us,' and we started walking towards Laverton, about twenty-eight miles. About halfway we could hear a truck in the distance so we shouted 'Get down!' and everybody dropped. We were well off the road so when the truck went past we lifted our heads and saw it was the mission truck.

Late in the afternoon we got to the Reserve turn-off

and we sat there, back from the road, for about fifteen minutes. While we were there the mission truck went past again with the three girls who had taken off the day before. They still didn't see us so we walked into the Reserve. The women came out to see whose kids were there and we stayed with relatives. I stayed with Aunty Lula who came and claimed me. She knew who I was but I didn't know her. Next day, one of the mothers went into Native Welfare and asked for rations for her child. Soon as he heard that, this Native Welfare officer jumped in his car and rounded us all up. Fancy asking Native Welfare for rations! Silly woman. Later, the first three girls said that they had told the missionary they could see little kids' tracks on the road. The driver had got off and looked at the tracks but he reckoned they were probably just women going hunting.

In the home, the missionaries belted us with a fan belt or a leather trouser belt. Sometimes I was belted with a cane at school. If you did something wrong they'd say, 'I'll belt the living daylights out of you!' I remember having welts and purple bruises on my legs. I can't remember what I did but we were punished for not answering the bell, or for climbing trees and tearing our clothes. Little things. Nothing serious. I remember girls wearing potato sacks. It was a punishment for doing things that the missionaries considered wrong. I think the missionaries took out their frustrations on the kids. Being in an isolated place would be hard for them. Maybe they were having trouble with children who were not adapting to their way of life. You can't just wipe Aboriginal ways and language out of a little child. So they were probably frustrated.

At Mount Margaret I was badly burned in a fire. I now know that the accident was on the eleventh of July 1958. It was very cold in the mornings and the missionaries had a room, we called it 'the shed', with an open fireplace. Every morning after breakfast the babies were brought in here to keep them warm. This morning I went to the dispensary for something and on my way back one of the girls told me to go to mind the babies while she went to the dispensary. I was sitting near the fire, warming myself, when one of the big girls called me to change out of my play clothes into my school clothes. That's the last thing I remember.

Some of the mission girls have told me that when I went outside, I burst into flames. They said I had a spark on me and it caught alight. They called out for help and Kathy, one of the big girls, ran to me and used her coat to smother out the flames. On the way to the little mission 'hospital' she tore off the burnt dress and put the coat back on me. But I can't remember any of that.

The first thing I remembered was someone trying to feed me boiled eggs, but I don't know if that was in Leonora Hospital or Perth. I remember the smell of the mattress in Princess Margaret Hospital. It had a funny smell to it that mattress. It was the smell of burnt skin and pus. The blankets were held by a frame so that they didn't touch me. I remember one of the doctors trying to get me to walk and holding out his hands for me to walk to him. But I remember just standing there. I could feel the blood trickling down my legs from the wounds, so they just put me back to bed. The smell sticks to you. That's what I remember most.

I don't remember much about Lucy Creeth Hospital in Perth except swimming in the pool for exercises. I remember getting excited about going back to Mount Margaret because, after all, I thought that was home. When I came back from Perth by train to the Malcolm Siding I saw the girls and Mr Jackson waiting for me. Later I was told that when we were back at Mount Margaret I hit my brother and told him off for not looking after me and not visiting me when I was in hospital.

After the accident I was like a 'freak show' in that mission. The missionaries wanted to see the scars. 'Come here, Rene, and lift up your dress,' they said. I was treated like a freak for anyone and everyone who came to the mission. Because of the scarring I couldn't sit up straight in school and I was always being hit with a ruler. Posture. Posture. I was hit in the back for bad posture. They didn't think that the scarring might be a problem, that the burn scars couldn't stretch. Even now I get pains at night from the tightness and can't get comfortable to sleep. There were no check-ups for me. The children could be cruel, too. If I had a disagreement with any of the girls I'd get, 'burnt this, burnt that, burnt everything else,' which was very painful. I had to strip naked for the big girls so they could see the scars. I'd cry for my mother who was hundreds of miles away, and I'd get, 'Go back to Warburton, you've got no mother here.' That's why I still cover up now — I never wear short clothes, or sleeveless things.

In the mission they drummed Christianity into us. The missionaries tried to shape and rule our lives in what they thought was the Christian way of living, preparing us to be domestic servants. We were only allowed to sing Christian songs, and the older girls had to go to Bible class and have prayer meetings. On Sundays we went to church morning and afternoon, Sunday school, and then a church meeting at night. We were always being reminded that Jesus loved us, but what I really wanted was my mother. We were just brainwashed little puppets.

Of all the children who were in Mount Margaret Mission of my age, only about four are still alive. We were led to believe that God would lead us through life. Sure we'd have temptations and Satan would lead us off the Christian path, but if we prayed and followed Jesus, he would help us. For most of us, it didn't work.

There wasn't much that was good in the mission, really. I liked the walks and the picnics, otherwise you were in the yard all the time. Holidays at Esperance were good but that was miles away from relations and home. One of the good things was athletics. Mount Margaret kids were always winning the local shield. Those kids were very good at athletics. I came to Perth once for athletics.

Some of us were picked to go to Leederville for the school carnival. We stayed at Bennett House in East Perth. We had to practise starting blocks and wear a little skirt. I was very self-conscious then. And nervous. We had never been in such a big crowd of people.

After ten years at Mount Margaret I went to Kurrawang Mission, run by the Gospel Brethren. I was there for three years. There were a few differences from Mount Margaret Mission — trees and landscape for one thing, but I prefer the desert and the mulga country. On Sundays and whenever we went to church, every female had to wear a hat or scarf. At Mount Margaret we didn't have to have our heads covered. At Kurrawang they had a tennis court and trampoline. Some days we would play day and night. I ran away from there, too.

We had supper one night and all the younger ones were in bed. On the spur of the moment someone said, 'Let's go to Kalgoorlie!' There were three of us. We bundled our blankets into a heap under the quilt like bodies and told one other girl to turn the lights out so when the missionary came to check she'd think we were all there. Anyhow, we took off and headed down to the main road. We thumbed a lift on the main road with an oldish man and his grandson who were going in to the pictures. We jumped off in Hannan Street and we were walking down Porter Street when we saw this policeman, so we headed into the darker part of town. One of the girls was turning around to check on that policeman and she walked straight into a tree.

She hit her head, and there was blood running down her face. After that she wanted to go back. So we stood there arguing about going back to Kurrawang. In the end we felt sorry for her and headed back down the Coolgardie road. We slept the night under a peppercorn tree — no blankets and freezing.

Next day we walked back to Kurrawang. We were sent to the missionaries' house and brought in one by one and questioned. This missionary was a big bloke, and he gave us the cane. My hands had welts and were swollen for days. His wife made us a cup of tea and they told us to play tennis on the lawn until the school bus came back. We pretended to play, but we couldn't even hold the racquets, our hands were so sore.

The only people living at Kurrawang were missionaries, the children and old Aboriginal people who lived on the Reserve. No parents or relatives visited, as they had at Mount Margaret. There was one girl boarding at Kurrawang and every school holiday and Christmas she went back to Leonora. The three years I was there we went down to Esperance for a few weeks every Christmas. All the children went. We didn't see any mothers with pieces of paper with their children's names on them.

If the missionaries saw you sitting on the ground telling stories, they said, 'Stop flogging the ground. You are not at Mount Margaret now, sit on the grass!' And we were told to forget speaking any language other than English. Today the languages are taught in some towns and communities. I spoke Ngaanyatjarra when I was taken to Mount Margaret, but by the time I was sent to Kurrawang I had lost my language and was speaking English and a type of Aboriginal slang. At Kurrawang we were not allowed to speak in any language other than English. By the time I was sent to Esperance to work I had lost my language and my identity. The missionaries had brainwashed me. The missionaries were forever putting Aboriginal people down, as heathens, and children of the devil, trying to turn me against my own people. It worked. It was all I ever heard; there was nobody telling me anything different. No wonder everyone was confused about where they belonged.

At Kurrawang I had to go through the 'freak show' again. One of the missionaries told me that I would never have children because of the scarring. She wasn't satisfied with telling me once. She said everything was God's plan. I don't think it was God's plan. That was just her idea of God. It's not mine. What sort of God would want that for a child? What sort of God would want a child to be burned and scarred? God had nothing to do with it.

Today, if we speak out about the treatment and conditions in the homes we were in, we are told that we should be grateful for being saved from the life of heathens. Sometimes I think that the government and the missionaries were trying to play God to a people they didn't understand. We were a people who lived with nature and loved and cared for the land. Our idea of God was very different.

The main aim of the missionaries was to convert us to

their religion and to teach reading and writing for work after the mission. Some people benefited from the missionaries' education, but lots more were just trained to be domestic servants on low-paid wages, like me. After Kurrawang I was sent even farther away from my family and country in the hope that I would forget them. I lost a grandmother's and parents' love and guidance, family life, extended family, language. Everything.

Even if some people benefited from the education, it didn't prepare any of us for racism outside the mission. Maybe they were thinking more about life after death than this life. They used to say, 'God will help you through life's temptations. If you read the Bible, pray and go to church you will be a shining example to the unconverted.' And, if you did these things, you'd be rewarded when you died.

That's what they said. But when I walked down the street in Esperance, people went right out of their way to walk around me instead of keeping to their straight path.

Abridged from *Rene Baker File #28 / E.D.P*
Rene Powell and Bernadette Kennedy, 2005.

Sally Morgan

A BLACK GRANDMOTHER

On 14 February 1966, Australia's currency changed from pounds, shilling and pence to dollars and cents. According to Mum and Nan, it was a step backwards. 'There's no money like the old money,' Nan maintained, and Mum agreed. They were shocked when they heard that our new money would not have as much silver in it as the old two-shilling, one-shilling, sixpence and threepence.

'It'll go bad, Glad,' said Nan one night, 'you wait and see. You can't make money like that, it'll turn green.'

Then I noticed that Nan had a jar on the shelf in the kitchen with a handful of two-shilling pieces in it. Towards the end of the week, the jar was overflowing with silver coins. I could contain my curiosity no longer.

'What are you saving up for, Nan?'

'Nothin'! Don't you touch any of that money!'

I cornered Mum in the bath. 'Okay Mum, why is Nan

hoarding all that money? You're supposed to hand it over to the bank and get new money.'

'Don't you say anything to anyone about that money, Sally. It's going to be valuable one day; we're saving it for you kids. When it's worth a lot we'll sell it and you kids can have what we make. You might need it by then.'

I went back in the kitchen. 'Mum told me what you're up to,' I told Nan. 'I think it's crazy.'

'Hmph! We don't care what you think, you'll be glad of it in a few years' time. Now you listen, if anyone from the government comes round asking for money, you tell them we gave all ours to the bank. If they pester you about the old money, you just tell 'em we haven't got money like that in this house.'

'Nan,' I half-laughed, 'no one from the government is gunna come round and do that!'

'Ooh, don't you believe it. You don't know what the government's like. You're too young. You'll find out one day what they can do to people. You never trust anybody who works for the government. You mark my words, Sally.'

I was often puzzled by the way Mum and Nan approached anyone in authority, as if they were frightened. I knew that couldn't be the reason, why on earth would anyone be frightened of the government?

Apart from art and English, I failed nearly everything else in the second term of my third year in high school. And

Mum was disgusted with my seven per cent for geometry and trigonometry.

'You've got your Junior soon. How on earth do you expect to pass that?'

'I don't care whether I pass or not. Why don't you let me leave school?'

'You'll leave school over my dead body!'

'What's the point in all this education if I'm going to spend the rest of my life drawing and painting?'

'You are not going to spend the rest of your life doing that, there's no future in it. Artists only make money after they're dead and gone.'

I gave up arguing and retreated to my room. Mum never took my ambition to be an artist seriously. Not that she didn't encourage me to draw. Once when I was bored, she had let me paint pictures all over the asbestos sheets that covered in our back verandah. Nan had thought it was real good.

I sighed. Nan believed in my drawings.

The following weekend, my Aunty Judy came to lunch. She was a friend of Mum's. Her family, the Drake-Brockmans, and ours had known each other for years. 'Sally, I want to have a talk with you about your future,' she said quietly, after we'd finished dessert.

I glared at Mum.

'You know you can't be an artist. They don't get anywhere in this world. You shouldn't worry your mother like that. She wants you to stay at school and finish your

Leaving. You can give up all idea of art school because it's just not on.'

I was absolutely furious. Not because of anything Aunty Judy had said, but because Mum had the nerve to get someone from outside the family to speak to me. Mum walked around looking guilty for the rest of the afternoon.

It wasn't only Mum and Aunty Judy, it was my art teacher at school as well. He held up one of my drawings in front of the class one day and pointed out everything wrong with it. There was no perspective; I was the only one with no horizon line. My people were flat and floating. You had to turn it on the side to see what half the picture was about. On and on he went. By the end of ten minutes the whole class was laughing and I felt very small. I always believed that drawing was my only talent; now I knew I was no good at that, either.

The thought of that horrible day made me want to cry. I was glad I was in my room and on my own, because I suddenly felt tears rushing to my eyes and spilling down my cheeks. I decided then to give up drawing. I was sick of banging my head against a brick wall. I got together my collection of drawings and paintings, sneaked down to the back of the yard, and burnt them.

When Mum and Nan found out what I'd done, they were horrified.

'All those beautiful pictures,' Nan moaned, 'gone for ever.' Mum just glared at me. I knew she felt she couldn't say too much. After all, she was partly responsible for driving me to it.

It took about a month for Mum and I to make up. She insisted that if I did my Junior, she wouldn't necessarily make me go on to my Leaving. Like a fool, I believed her.

Towards the end of the school year, I arrived home early one day to find Nan sitting at the kitchen table, crying. I froze in the doorway. I'd never seen her cry before.

'Nan ... what's wrong?'

'Nothin'!'

'Then what are you crying for?'

She lifted up her arm and thumped her clenched fist hard on the kitchen table. 'You bloody kids don't want me, you want a bloody white grandmother, I'm black. Do you hear, black, black, black!' With that, Nan pushed back her chair and hurried out to her room. I continued to stand in the doorway, I could feel the strap of my heavy schoolbag cutting into my shoulder, but I was too stunned to remove it.

For the first time in my fifteen years, I was conscious of Nan's colouring. It was true, she wasn't white. Well, I thought logically, if she wasn't white, then neither were we. What did that make us, what did that make me? I had never thought of myself as being black before.

That night, as my sister Jill and I were lying quietly on our beds, looking at a poster of John, Paul, George and Ringo, I said, 'Jill ... did you know Nan was black?'

'Course I did.'

'I didn't, I just found out.'

'I know you didn't. You're really dumb, sometimes. God, you reckon I'm gullible, but some things you just don't see. You know we're not Indian, don't you?'

'Mum said we're Indian.'

'Does Nan look Indian?'

'I've never really thought about how she looks. Maybe she comes from some Indian tribe we don't know about.'

'Ha! That'll be the day! You know what we are, don't you?'

'No, what?'

'Boongs, we're Boongs!' I could tell Jill was unhappy with the idea.

It took a few minutes before I summoned up enough courage to say, 'What's a Boong?'

'You know, Aboriginal. God, of all things, we're Aboriginal!'

'Oh.' I suddenly understood. There was a great deal of social stigma attached to being Aboriginal at our school.

'I can't believe you've never heard the word Boong,' Jill muttered in disgust. 'Haven't you ever listened to the kids at school? If they want to run you down, they say, "Aah, ya just a Boong." Honestly, Sally, you live the whole of your life in a daze!'

Jill was right; I did live in a world of my own. She was much more attuned to our social environment. It was important for her to be accepted at school, because she enjoyed being there.

'You know, Jill,' I said after a while, 'if we are Boongs, and

I don't know if we are or not, but if we are, there's nothing we can do about it, so we might as well just accept it.'

'Accept it? Can you tell me one good thing about being an Abo?'

'Well, I don't know much about them,' I answered. 'They like animals, don't they? We like animals.'

'A lot of people like animals, Sally. Haven't you heard of the RSPCA?'

'Of course I have! But don't Abos feel close to the earth and all that stuff?'

'God, I don't know. All I know is none of my friends like them. I've been trying to convince Lee for two years that we're Indian.' Lee was Jill's best friend and her opinions were very important. Lee loved Nan, so I didn't see that it mattered.

'You know Susan?' Jill said, interrupting my thoughts. 'Her mother said she doesn't want her mixing with you because you're a bad influence. She reckons all Abos are a bad influence.'

'Aaah, I don't care about Susan, never liked her much anyway.'

'You still don't understand, do you,' Jill groaned in disbelief. 'It's a terrible thing to be Aboriginal. Nobody wants to know you, not just Susan. You can be Indian, Dutch, Italian, anything, but not Aboriginal! I suppose it's all right for someone like you, you don't care what people think. You don't need anyone, but I do!' Jill pulled her rugs over her head and pretended she'd gone to sleep. I think she was crying, but I had too much new information to think about to try and comfort her. Besides, what could I say?

Nan's outburst over her colouring and Jill's assertion that we were Aboriginal heralded a new phase in my relationship with my mother. I began to pester her incessantly about our background. Mum consistently denied Jill's assertion. She even told me that Nan had come out on a boat from India in the early days. In fact, she was so convincing I began to wonder if Jill was right after all.

When I wasn't pestering Mum, I was busy pestering Nan. To my surprise, I discovered that Nan had a real short fuse when it came to talking about the past. Whenever I attempted to question her, she either lost her temper and began to accuse me of all sorts of things, or she locked herself in her room and wouldn't emerge until it was time for Mum to come home from work. It was a conspiracy.

One night, Mum came into my room and sat on the end of my bed. She had her This Is Serious look on her face. With an unusual amount of firmness in her voice, she said quietly, 'Sally, I want to talk to you.'

I lowered my *Archie* comic. 'What is it?'

'I think you know. Don't act dumb with me. You're not to bother Nan any more. She's not as young as she used to be and your questions are making her sick. She never knows when you're going to try and trick her. There's no point in digging up the past; some things are better left buried. Do you understand what I'm saying? You're to leave her alone.'

'Okay, Mum,' I replied glibly, 'but on one condition.'

'What's that?'

'You answer one question for me.'

'What is it?' Poor Mum, she was a trusting soul.

'Are we Aboriginal?'

Mum snorted in anger and stormed out. Jill chuckled from her bed. 'I don't know why you keep it up. I think it's better not to know for sure, that way you don't have to face up to it.'

'I keep pestering them because I want to know the truth, and I want to hear it from Mum's own lips.'

'It's a lost cause, they'll never tell you.'

'I'll crack 'em one day.'

Jill shrugged good-naturedly and went back to reading her *True Romance* magazine.

I settled back into my mattress and began to think about the past. Were we Aboriginal? I sighed and closed my eyes. A mental picture flashed vividly before me. I was a little girl again, and Nan and I were squatting in the sand near the back steps.

'This is a track, Sally. See how they go.' I watched, entranced, as she made the pattern of a kangaroo. 'Now, this is a goanna and here are emu tracks. You see, they all different. You got to know all of them if you want to catch tucker.'

'That's real good, Nan.'

'You want me to draw you a picture, Sal?' she said as she picked up a stick.

'Okay.'

'These are men, you see, three men. They are very quiet. They're hunting. Here are kangaroos; they're listening, waiting. They'll take off if they know you're coming.' Nan wiped the sand picture out with her hand. 'It's your turn now,' she said, 'you draw something.'

I grasped the stick eagerly. 'This is Jill and this is me. We're going down the swamp.' I drew some trees and bushes ...

I opened my eyes and the picture vanished. Had I remembered something important? I didn't know. That was the trouble. I knew nothing about Aboriginal people. I was clutching at straws.

It wasn't long before I was too caught up in my preparation for my Junior examinations to bother too much about where we'd come from. At that time the Junior was the first major exam in high school. To a large extent, it determined your future. If you failed, you automatically left school and looked for a job. If you passed, it was generally accepted that you would do another two years' study and aim for university entrance.

Mum was keen on me doing well, so I decided that, for her, I'd make the effort and try and pass subjects I'd previously failed. For the first time in my school life, I actually sat up late, studying my textbooks. It was hard work, but Mum encouraged me by bringing in cups of tea and cake or toast and jam.

After each examination, she'd ask me anxiously how I'd gone. My reply was always, 'Okay.' I never really knew. Sometimes I thought I'd done all right, but then I reasoned that all I needed was a hard marker and I might fail. I didn't want to get Mum's hopes up.

Much to the surprise of the whole family, I passed every subject, even scoring close to the distinction mark in English and art. Mum was elated.

'I knew you could do it. Mr Buddee was right about you.'

Good old Mr Buddee. I didn't know whether to curse or thank him. Now that I had passed my Junior, I sensed that there was no hope of Mum allowing me to leave school. I should have deliberately failed, I thought. Then she wouldn't have had any choice. Actually, I had considered just that, but for some reason I couldn't bring myself to do it. I guess it was my pride again.

Abridged from *My Place*
Sally Morgan, 1987.

Tjalaminu Mia
BOORN — TAPROOT

When I look back on my life I can see experiences that have my own mark of choice on them, and experiences that were way beyond my control. This is because half of my life was lived in a state of oppression, while the other half has been spent rediscovering who I really am. The road to self discovery has been long and traumatic because I was taken away from my family and culture and institutionalised. This hasn't stopped me from delving back into my taproots though. I've embraced the challenge in order to understand myself and my life better.

The taproot is the root of the tree that goes the deepest. In my family, taproots are really important because, as my mother always says, 'We didn't get here by ourselves. We have others to thank for that and we should acknowledge it.'

One of the taproots in my family was Great Grandma Minnie Knapp Keen-Hayward, who was a dainty sort of woman. Her mother was a traditional Nyungar woman from the Great Southern region of Western Australia. Her father was a whitefella called Charles Knapp. Although quite young, I still have a faint memory of Great Grannie Minnie staying with us when we lived in Tambellup, which is a small town in the south-west.

I was a bit forward as a child and with this came an interest in my extended family, so I was always asking questions. Whenever anyone came to the front gate, which I would be swinging on, and ask for my mum, I'd say. 'Who are you? Are you coming to stay with us? Have you brought me any lollies?' Even though I was like this, the oldies didn't seem to mind. They thought highly of me and knew and loved me as Beryl's oldest girl and Len and Em's grandkid.

I was around four or five years old when Great Grannie Minnie used to visit and because she didn't come around much there were lots of hugs and kisses when she did, which I lapped up. I would take her hand and walk with her up the steps to our house and get a cushion for her to sit on because sometimes she liked to sit on the floor. Then out would come the cigarettes. She'd unroll them, rub the tobacco in her hands, then pop it into her mouth and chew it. Sometimes she'd sit in our lounge room beside the fire and she had a tin cup which was affectionately known in our house as 'Grannie Hayward's spitting cup'. To my delight she'd occasionally spit into the flames and make them flare up the chimney, but she'd only do that if Mum wasn't watching.

My mother took good care of Gran. She always made sure there was plenty of wood for the fire when Gran was coming, because it was real cold in that part of country. She also stocked up on tea, sugar, damper and treacle, because that's what Gran liked.

Mum was good at making people feel welcome. She's always been there to give family members a helping hand, and has been especially good to the oldies. Family members would often say, 'If you need anything, Ber's here ...' She was known for making sure the old fellas were looked after at family gatherings, and she kept her door open for them to stay with us and put their feet up when they needed a bit of peace and quiet.

Granny Hayward's oldest child, who was my grandfather on my mother's side, became another important taproot in our family. His name was Lennard George Keen, and he was a grandfather any child would be delighted to call their pop. He was a very loving, gentle person and he never raised his voice to growl at us, but then we respected him so much he didn't have to. When we worked on farms Dada Keen would come and spend time with us, taking us out rabbit trapping, mallee root picking, snaring kangaroos along the fence line and picking wool off dead sheep for pocket money. He even taught us games to play in the open paddocks that surrounded our house.

He'd get us to stand in a line on the rise of a small hill, where we'd each have an old car tyre at the side of us. What we had to do was run with it alongside us, hitting it with our hand. The first one to get to the bottom of the hill and touch the fence was the winner. If you fell over and were left behind, usually on the ground laughing your head off, and the tyre went rolling away in its own direction, or if it got to the fence line before you, you lost. The winner would get threepence next time we went to town for our stores, but Grandad would give the losers the same amount so no one felt left out. You could buy a lot for threepence in those days.

Dada Keen was a patient person and I really liked to follow him around, watching what he was doing and asking him questions about everything. He always took the time to stop and explain things to me and I think he liked having someone young in tow, so we enjoyed each other's company.

Sometimes when he was visiting we'd have a cook-up outside and us kids would help him to make a big fire. Then we'd arrange our stumps around the fire so we could sit and listen to him tell us stories about our culture. He'd talk about the animals, the land, the waterways, the stars and how we were all connected. He used to say that Aboriginal people could feel the land's pulse. All that we had to do was be very quiet, close our eyes, and put our bare feet on the ground. Then we'd feel the land's heartbeat. He also told us that we needed to respect all these things, as well as the old people who'd gone back to spirit. He talked about the hardships they'd had to endure, but he also told us to have pride in who we are. He told us about the birds too.

He always knew when it was going to rain. 'It's going to rain soon,' he'd say, 'the rainbird is calling out to us.' When I asked him how he knew, he'd reply. 'Well, the spirits have sent that rainbird along to tell us to get movin' and get our jobs done because there's gunna be a downpour any time now.' Sure enough, it'd rain. I never forgot that bird. Years later, when I heard it calling out, I'd say to my own kids, 'It's going to rain.' And it always did.

Grandad also told us to go by our gut feelings, especially when we were out in the bush. When he was a young boy he looked after sheep and in those days the bush was very thick and could be dangerous, especially with those little hairy fellas who Nyungar people call woodatchis, running around. He said not to be afraid, but to be watchful of where you were and what was going on around you. 'Remember what I'm tell'n you because this is a part of who you are, it's your culture and I don't want you to forget it. Always remember this my girl.' He gave us kids a lot of cultural teaching, but sadly our lives wouldn't stay like that.

It wasn't long before my brothers and sisters and I were put into Sister Kate's Children's Home. Sister Kate's was set up by the Native Welfare Department in the 1930s. Its aim was to turn lighter skinned Aboriginal kids into white citizens and I suppose it was part of what used to be called the White Australia Policy, because the politicians of the day wanted this land to be white. It was a very racist policy because they expected us to forget all about our families and our culture and take our place in white society instead.

I became rebellious in the Home. I was fed a diet of Western religion, which I always questioned, so I was often in trouble. 'You are a wilful, disrespectful child and a bad influence on the other children.' That's what they liked to tell me because they didn't like me challenging what they were teaching.

'Why can't you tell us stories about other spiritual beings besides Jesus and the Holy Ghost?' I used to ask them. I wanted to hear stories like the ones Grandad used to tell.

'Your grandfather made all that up,' they told me. 'Your family don't really care about you or your brothers and sisters.'

They played a game of divide and conquer with all the Aboriginal families who had kids in there.

'If you don't stop questioning us you'll be punished and the other children in your cottage won't get their weekly ration of sweets. So stop misbehaving!'

This went on and on until I learned to shut up and keep my thoughts to myself. I had to suppress my knowledge of the cultural stories I'd heard and just listen to their Christian ones.

This meant that while I was there, something very deep was missing in my life and it was that deep sense of being connected to my people, my family, my ancestors and to our cultural beliefs. It was a spirituality the Sunday School teachers couldn't understand and because of this oppression I started to lose my sense of being a Nyungar kid. The Home took away our sense of self worth and we didn't know where we fitted in the world anymore. I wasn't going out bush with Grandad looking for bush tucker, and he wasn't showing me the animal markings on the ground and how to track them. I wasn't involved in the cultural things that gave me a sense of place and a deep spiritual understanding of who I really was. I lost all this when we were placed in the institution, and it led to a lot of self-destructive behaviour later. It was a long time before me and my brothers and sisters sorted ourselves out.

While there were mostly bad times for me at Sister Kate's, there were a few good times too. Like when the kids from various state orphanages got together at the Zoo, the Royal Show, the pictures, or Peters Ice Cream Factory. It was great having a chance to meet up with other kids in the same situation and let off some steam. Those times were fun and loud and our ears would be ringing for hours afterwards. Imagine being stuck in His Majesty's Theatre with hundreds of screaming kids from institutions like Sister Kate's, Castledare, Clontarf, the Mt Lawley Receiving Home and the Salvation Army Boys and Girls Homes.

Still, even though they were fun times, if an outsider was looking in on us all they'd be thinking: where are all these kids' parents and why aren't the kids with them? All any of us really wanted was our families.

Dada Keen only visited us once that I can remember when we were in the Home. This wasn't because he didn't want to; it was because they used to stop people at the gate so we couldn't mix up with our families. This made the whole situation even harder for us. By the time we all left Sister Kate's and the Salvation Army Boys and Girls Homes, we were teenagers, and a lot of damage had been done to our family connections. We went into the Home together as a family, but we didn't come out as one. At Sister Kate's we were separated and put in different cottages, so even as brothers and sisters we hadn't lived together as a family for years. When we came out we had to adjust and Mum had to adjust too.

One by one we made our way back to our mother, uncles, aunties and grandparents. But a lot of things had changed. I've never asked my brothers and sisters, especially my older siblings, how they felt about suddenly being last in line in a group of cousins for our grandparents' attention, when before they'd been the first.

Some of the last meaningful times I had with my grandfather were when I visited him in hospital. I remember once when I was sitting quietly on the bed holding his hand as he slept, but then he suddenly woke up and looked at me and smiled. I saw an amazing thing. In his blue eyes I saw a young soul. And that's how I remember him and his beautiful spirit.

After Sister Kate's I went into the Salvation Army Girls Home until just after my fourteenth birthday. By then the people in charge all agreed I was very disruptive so I think they were glad to get rid of me. I'd run away a few times looking for Mum and they were sick of having to deal with the result.

The last time I made a run for it was at night. I kissed my two sisters goodbye and asked two older girls to keep an eye on them while I was gone. Then I jumped out of the window of the girls dormitory, made my way down the back of the Home and jumped over the back fence. I headed to my girlfriend's house from school, where I slept in her chook pen for the night and early next morning she gave me some food to hold me over. Though I looked a bit the worse for wear and was a bit high on the nose from the chook poo, I didn't care. I was 'on a mission' and I was not going to let anything or anyone stop me. I walked along the railway line till I reached Perth, where I made my way to my aunty's house. My mother's sister gave me a feed and a couple of cool drink bottles to cash in at the local shops for a train fair to Midland. When I hopped the old 'dogbox' I was scared stiff that I was going to be pulled up by one of the train guards because I was just a kid and he would've known I should be in school. Every time the train pulled into a station, I'd put my head out of the small window just enough to see where the guards were before I felt safe to continue. When I got to Midland I kept my wits about me because you had to be careful when you were on the run as a kid, as there were many dangers that could befall you.

I kept to the back streets, making my way from the Midland train station to my grandparents' house in Midvale, ducking the 'Bunjii men' and 'rock spiders' — I think the words used now are sleazy old men and paedophiles — that prowled the streets looking to take advantage of anyone young and innocent. I'd learned the hard facts of life early, so I knew I had to protect myself. I also kept low because the police seemed to have an innate radar when it came to spotting runaways and I didn't want to get picked up before I even got to my granny's house. If I got caught too soon, it would've all been for nothing.

The trouble was, when I finally did arrive, I was made to go back again. It upset Mum and my grandparents to do that but they were worried my running away would work against my mother, as well as my younger brothers and sisters, in finally getting back together again as a family.

Mum and one of my younger aunties walked me into Midland to the police station and left me there. Mum mouthed 'I love you,' and then she was gone. I felt so alone and angry, so I started to cheek the old police sergeant and a woman officer who were on duty. The old boy looked at me from over the rim of his glasses with a bit of a scowl on his face, but the woman officer had sorrow and sympathy in her eyes, which made me feel kaarna — real shame for my behaviour. So I stopped swinging around in the swivel chair, kept my mouth shut and just sooked quietly till they drove me back to the Home.

Matron met us on the steps and was very nice to the police and not too bad towards me either. I think they'd already decided I wouldn't be there much longer. My punishment was to polish the long walkway in the entry hall of the turn-of-the-century mansion we lived in. It took me all night, on my hands and knees, and I still had to go to school the next day and by then I hadn't really slept for twenty-four hours.

Not long after that they let me go. I was happy to finally leave, but sad too because my two sisters weren't coming with me. They were still stuck there. When I got out I lived with a few different family members because Mum had to work away in the bush to make enough money to get a decent house and furnish it to the Welfare's standards. All that had to be done before we could all be together again as a proper family.

The kind of institutionalisation that I and my brothers and sisters experienced as children doesn't prepare you for life, it just prepares you for more institutionalisation. A lot of the kids from homes ended up as prison inmates and this included my own brothers. They graduated from the homes to stints in various institutions for youth, and finally into maximum security prison for men. They were on a treadmill of hopelessness, of feeling beaten before their lives had even begun, and that all started at Sister Kate's. They'd been deprived of basic human rights as a child, and as they grew older they were harassed by various government officials, especially the police. It wasn't easy for them to turn their lives around. I ended up in prison too, but not as a prisoner. I was one of the first Aboriginal women to work in the prison system with our people.

It took years for my brothers to find happiness, but they are an inspiration to me now and I feel very proud of them and how they've come through all the hard times.

Abridged from *Speaking from the Heart*
edited by Sally Morgan, Tjalaminu Mia and
Blaze Kwaymullina, 2007.

Kim Scott

OF ABORIGINAL DESCENT

My father, Tommy Scott, was the only surviving child to an Aboriginal woman who died when he was ten years old, after which his Aboriginal grandmother continued to raise him until his Scottish father arranged boarding schools and even a succession of stepmothers. He still occasionally saw his grandmother. Sometimes, too, an aunty or uncle looked after him.

When I was a child my father told me to be proud I was 'of Aboriginal descent'. Perhaps it was the silence surrounding his words that made them resonate as they did; I'd certainly heard no such thing anywhere else in my life, certainly not in my reading or schooling. There didn't seem much in the way of empirical evidence to support my father's words. A child, and unable to either calibrate injustice and racism or identify its cause, I sensed the legacy of oppression.

My father and I didn't have a lot of conversations, which is probably why I remember those we did have, like when — at six or seven years old — I came home bruised and bleeding and cursing two other Noongar boys — strangers — I'd clashed with after they'd stolen my younger brother's bicycle. 'Coons,' I was calling them.

My father shut me up. Don't talk that way, he said. People are people. And for the first time he told me to be proud I was 'of Aboriginal descent'.

Perhaps my father's words resonated so strangely simply because, in 1960s south-western Australia, it was hard to articulate pride in Aboriginality. My father wanted me to have something more like a faith, a psychological conviction. It was not something easily put into words. He said to be proud, that was the important thing, but he lacked the vocabulary, didn't have the right stories at hand. It's a continuing problem I think, this struggle to articulate the significance and energy of a specific Indigenous heritage.

In the mid 1960s it was put to me in terms of being proud to be 'of Aboriginal descent' and 'part-Aboriginal', but not much more than ten years later I was a young adult living and working among Aboriginal people of south-western Australia — Noongars — who repeatedly said, 'You can't be bit and bit. What are you, Noongar or wadjela?'

It was a political imperative about the need to commit, to align oneself with either white or black, and I felt compelled to obey. There didn't seem to be any choice, not if I wished to be among Noongars. But even as I winced at the phrase 'Aboriginal descent' and learned more of our shared history, our story of colonisation, I was not always confident of my acceptance by other Noongars.

My father died in his thirties. Young as he was, he was several years older than his mother had been at the time of her death.

I didn't grow up in the bush. There was no traditional upbringing of stories around the camp fire, no earnest transmission of cultural values. The floor of the first house I remember was only partially completed, and my three siblings and I, pretending we were tight-rope walkers, balanced on the floor-joists spanning the soft dirt and rubble half a metre below us.

We moved to a government house on a bitumen street with gutters running down each side, and even though the street came to an end, the slope ran on and on through patchy scrub and past the superphosphate factory, the rubbish tip, the Native Reserve.

Individuals were fined for being on the reserve, and fined for being in town. Their crime was being non-Aboriginal in the one place and Aboriginal in the other, after legislation was refined in the attempt to snare those who — as the frustrated bureaucrat put it — 'run with the hares and hunt with the hounds' and to trip them as they moved to and fro across a dividing legislative line.

My father was mobile that way, always moving.

From the city where he'd reached adulthood, he moved back close to the country of our Noongar ancestors, and worked on the roads as 'leading hand' in a gang of mainly Aboriginal men. Returning home after being away from us for ten days of every fortnight, he usually took us camping. He wanted to be a professional fisherman, and we rattled along the coast in a battered 4WD and trailed nets from a dinghy in the country of our countless ancestors, 'going home' together. We kids helped with the nets, cleaned fish, and even hawked them around the neighbourhood. My mother broke up blocks of ice with the back of an axe, and we carefully layered fish and ice into crates which my father then loaded onto a train bound for the city.

One among other Noongar and wadjela children running barefoot in a suburb a skip, hop and a step from the reserve, I was only ever at the fringe of a community which showed all the signs of being under siege.

My immediate family line didn't have the experience of reserves or missions. I don't know that sort of anger, can't claim the same sense of a collective identity forged by the experience of oppression. I knew something about the shame — just from being 'of Aboriginal descent' in the Australia I've known — and I knew something about the pride, if not how to adequately express and articulate it.

Abridged from *Kayang & Me*
Kim Scott and Hazel Brown, 2005.

Bronwyn Bancroft

CROSSING THE LINE

On the second of April 1949 a man and a woman crossed the line. One was black and one was white and they thought it would be all right.

My father was black. My mother was white. Racism was rife. It was a small country town called Tenterfield in the 1950s and times were hard. Bill Bancroft, my father, wasn't even an Australian citizen, yet he married my mother, a white woman whose name was Dorothy Moss. Who could question their courage, in particular Dorothy, who had everything to lose. It is the union of these two people that shows what is great about the human race — the desire to follow instinct. It didn't matter that one person had black skin. What mattered was they were in love. A love you can read of in fairytales — defying boundaries, defying doubters, defying the White Australia Policy. From this partnership I was born. My name is Bronwyn Bancroft and this is my story.

Born in 1958, I was the last of seven children. My eldest brothers and sisters were not that much older than me, as my mum had one child each year for eight years, but they used to say to visitors and other family members that Mum and Dad only had me to wear out the old clothes. The earliest memories I have are of lying under the kitchen table. I would rub my eyes then look around the room. The mist of tears distorted everything I saw. The tablecloth with the interwoven shapes took life. Everywhere I looked there were patterns.

It was as if I was born in another time, another place, another family. Like my brothers and sisters though, I woke to a world of inequality. I was in Tenterfield, New South Wales. Population: 3000. I was born not black, not white — an Aboriginal Australian.

In a small country town I was either going to be very creative or a lot of trouble. My different perspective would distance me from my siblings, not only because I was the last of seven children, but also because they came across a lot more racism than I did. One brother had many fights under the bridge after school when people called him a boong or a coon. I was saved from that because they cut a path of respect that I followed, blissfully unaware at the time of their trials and tribulations. I did not have to live daily through such horrendous moments. That's not to say

I haven't experienced racism. I have, and when it happens it always sends an arrow straight into my heart. I wonder what makes a person think they have the right to speak or act in such an inhumane way. I never understand it.

I think the lack of respect afforded to my siblings by some elements of a small country town pushed them into a place where they did not want to go. Challenged as Aboriginal people, they would have preferred to be treated as Australians, but they mostly succumbed to the tweener world, where whites never accepted you and neither did blacks. You were caught in that vacuous space in between. I never wanted to be a tweener. I knew I couldn't live like that. I was Aboriginal and I was extremely proud of my dad. I embraced my Aboriginality wholeheartedly and my identity became the whole focal point for my life and for what I later taught my children.

I was fortunate in that throughout my life I had much greater social freedom than my brothers and sisters. When I was nine years old, the 1967 referendum voted in favour of including Indigenous people in the census, which effectively recognised our citizenship. When I was fourteen years old, the 1972 Tent Embassy was set up outside Parliament House, Canberra, to protest against the treatment of Indigenous Australians in this country. I was born into a generation of change and I embraced that too. I came to understand how important and meaningful my identity was for me. It was so much more than a name and a family. It was a belief, a deep sense of spirituality, a lifestyle and it meant that I also opened my arms to my ancestral land from an early age.

I always loved going to the bush at Lionsville, where my father's family are the traditional custodians of the land. I enjoyed the sanctity of the bush kingdom and felt a freedom there like no other place. Without over-romanticising, I really felt that when I set foot on our land a weight was lifted from me. It was like that feeling you get when you arrive home after a long day at school carrying around a bag full of heavy books. Walking into your room, you fling the bag down on the floor. Without the weight you feel immediately stronger. The bed beckons. You lie down and are momentarily free from everything that weighs you down. That's how I felt in Lionsville. I even loved the drive there, crammed into the back of the old Ford with my brothers and sisters. The road from Tenterfield was mainly dirt. I remember looking out the back at the dust exploding behind us. The road took us past Tabulam, and Baryulgil, then on to this remote area called Lionsville. All of us kids were on the lookout for the three big hills. When we saw them we knew our destination was just ahead. Hill one, two, and three passed. We were here. We were excited. It was time to get to the creek.

The creek was out the back of our grandfather's place. We were so happy to arrive after being crammed together in the truck, in the heat and dust, and we would rush straight down to the creek. There were catfish in the water, but we were careful not to disturb their nest. Diving off the fallen log into the pristine waters of the Washpool Creek — what a divine moment. Laughter and excitement and the thrill of eating fresh fish and homemade bread by nightfall.

What I felt more than anything was the sense of peace and space that this bush hideaway offered. I loved the little tin cubby nestling under the giant crepe myrtle with its own little stove and playthings. It was my retreat.

Then, after we were sent to bed, you could hear the old people telling stories. Our beds were on the front verandah, and we listened in as much as we could. I loved being able to fall asleep in the company of adults while they related the day's events. I never heard anyone speak about racism. Ignorance is bliss, especially when you are a child. As my eyes started to close I would look at and listen to the world beyond the verandah. You could hear the frogs in the galvanised pipe bars that made the front fence, and see the stars lining the interior of the night sky ... the saucepan ... the three sisters. The stars always made me think about how Dad and Uncle Pat would say that these signposts in the sky were their compasses when they were out doing jobs for their dad, my grandfather. All this created a sense of home. I was enchanted with the knowledge that I was walking on the same land as my grandmother's mother and her mother. Walking the land allowed me to connect spiritually to my ancestors. As young as I was, I knew even then that this was the ultimate in personal freedom.

I am descended from Aboriginal, English, Polish and Scottish. My father always used to say, 'You are what you are and nothing else!' and I thought this was an interesting and perceptive statement from a black man who felt that he was surrounded by inequality. I did not have a chance to meet all my great grandparents but I knew they existed as a part of me.

People always ask me why I identify as an Aboriginal person with this mixed up ancestry. It is important to note that in Australia you are either recognised as an Aboriginal person or you are not. I am descended from the best people in this country: smart, resilient and survivors. Why would I not want to recognise my own family? Also, I live in Australia, not Scotland or Poland or England, and as such I feel the heartbeat of my Old People. I feel the resonance of their lives and their times and this is what guides me, and in them I trust.

I am proud of who I am. I am proud of where I've come from. I am proud of what I've done and I'm proud of where I'm going. I am a Bundjalung woman who sees each new day as the beginning of the rest of my life. You can't change the past, but you can live a different future.

Abridged from *Speaking from the Heart*
edited by Sally Morgan, Tjalaminu Mia and
Blaze Kwaymullina, 2007.

BIOGRAPHICAL NOTES

BRONWYN BANCROFT was born in 1958 and belongs to the Bundjalung people of Northern New South Wales. She is a well-known painter and is also interested in the environment and teaching other people the joy of creating art.

ALICE BILARI SMITH was born at Rocklea Station in the Pilbara in 1928. Her mother was a Banyjima woman and her father was a white teamster. She was raised by her Aboriginal family and, although she did not know it at the time, narrowly escaped being removed to Moore River. After marriage to Bulluru Jack Smith, Alice lived in the bush and raised a large family before settling in Roebourne so that her children could attend school.

HAZEL BROWN is the senior elder of a large, extended Noongar family. She has worked as a rural labourer, was a member of Western Australia's first Metropolitan Commission of Elders, and is a registered Native Title claimant over part of the south coast of Western Australia.

JUKUNA MONA CHUGUNA was a young woman when she walked out of the desert with her husband. They worked on cattle stations for a number of years, then moved to the mission at Fitzroy Crossing in the early 1970s. Jukuna was among the first women to attend Walmajarri literacy classes and worked on Walmajarri projects with linguists. She has travelled widely in Australia and overseas to exhibit her paintings.

ERIC HEDLEY HAYWARD is a Noongar Elder from south-west Western Australia. He hails from a family of leaders in sport. Eric has continued his family's contribution by promoting Aboriginal community sport, particularly football and golf, for which he has coordinated state and local events. He is currently completing a Doctor of Philosophy at Curtin University.

STEPHEN KINNANE is a descendant through his mother's mother of the Miriwoong people of the East Kimberley and was raised in Noongar country in the south-west of Western Australia. He is the author of *Shadow Lines* (2003); collaborated with Lauren Marsh and Alice Nannup on the book *When the Pelican Laughed* (1992) and co-wrote and co-produced a documentary, *The Coolbaroo Club* (1996).

TJALAMINU MIA is a Nyungar woman with bloodline links to the Minang and Goreng peoples of the south-west of

Western Australia. She works as a research fellow in oral history and the arts in the School of Indigenous Studies at The University of Western Australia.

SALLY MORGAN was born in Perth in 1951. She has published books for both adults and children, including her acclaimed autobiography, *My Place*. She has a national reputation as an artist and has works in many private and public collections.

ALICE NANNUP was born on a Pilbara station in 1911 to an Aboriginal mother and white father. She was taken from her community at the age of twelve and sent south to work as a domestic servant. After her marriage in 1932, Alice raised ten children. Known as 'Nan', she lived in Geraldton surrounded by her friends and extensive family until she passed away in November 1995.

MAY L O'BRIEN *BEM* was born in the Eastern Goldfields of Western Australia, and at the age of five was taken to Mount Margaret Mission where she spent the next twelve years. May is a long-standing statesperson within Aboriginal and Torres Strait Islander education. She has lived and worked within Aboriginal education systems for more than four decades and, although officially retired, continues to be an active advocate for improving the educational outcomes of Aboriginal and Torres Strait Islander children.

RENE POWELL was born in 1948 in the Warburton Ranges, in the Central Desert of Western Australia. Her people are the Ngaanyatjarra. Removed from her family at the age of four, she grew up at Mount Margaret Mission and then Kurrawang Mission where she was trained for domestic work. Most of her adult life was spent in Perth until, after the death of her husband, she went back to Warburton to live and start a garden.

KIM SCOTT is a descendant of people living along the south coast of Western Australia prior to colonisation, and is proud to be one among those who call themselves Noongar. Kim's most recent novel, *That Deadman Dance*, won the Miles Franklin Award, along with a number of other literary awards and prizes. He is currently Professor of Writing at Curtin University in Western Australia.

DAVID SIMMONS was born in Perth to parents from the Nyoongar language group of far-south Western Australia but has lived and worked in Roebourne for most of his adult life.

JOAN WINCH was born in 1935 and belongs to the Nyungar and Martujarra people of Western Australia. She is a well-known fighter for Aboriginal rights and was awarded the World Health Organization's Sasakawa Award in 1987 for her work on Indigenous primary health care.

LOLA YOUNG was born on Rocklea Station in the Pilbara in 1942 to Aboriginal parents. At an early age she went with her grandparents to learn Aboriginal bush medicine and culture. Her working life started at the age of about ten and when she turned fourteen she was given away in marriage. Lola established the Wakuthuni Community in 1990 to bring her people back home to their country. She taught Aboriginal culture, bush medicine and bush tucker to both black and white people until her death in 2010.